EXPRESSIONS FOR IMPRESSIONS

Expressions for Impressions

How to Make Colorful Card Creations
That Inspire

STEVEN GARRETT

Contents

Dedication

I dedicate this book to my Mother and Wife the two Ladies that give me love, hope, and
inspiration.
Showing me that love is real and they truly bring happiness and light
to my life where before there was only
darkness and doubt!

Introduction

My name Steven Garrett I was recently released on parole in which I was incarcerated in Texas. I was serving a ten year sentence on a drug conviction. I wrote this book while I was incarcerated because I could never get a card through the commissary that truly conveyed the message that I was trying to express to those I love. I also found out that a card I took the time to create with my own two hands were not only more appealing to the eye, but were more heartfelt because they were hand made. no one can convey what you want to express to those you love better than you can yourself. It is your thoughts and feelings and you know those better than anyone else.

So as we go through this journey of creating colorful creations you will learn to confidently create beautiful, warm, and heartfelt creations. Even those who can not draw can create cards that when sent to those you love, will appreciate more than anything you can buy. Because you took the time and energy to create something to let them know you love them.

When I started making cards at the facility I was at they wouldn't even allow me to have a pencil much less colored pencils, markers, or colors of any kind. I learned that if you have desire to do something you will find a way to get it done. So I had a desire to impress my loved ones with my expressions. So I was determined to create cards to send to my loved ones. With limited resources. So I made stencils of hearts, stars, and clouds. I made the stencils out of card board and the backs of legal pads. I bought an art pad off of commissary. I then got a rag a stick of deodorant and a magazine. Then with these materials I started making cards to send my wife and family that they still have to this day.

I have come along way from those days. Let me explain what I did real quick so you won't think I am a nut job. If you take a rag and wrap it around your finger, and then run it over the top of your deodorant it will act as a solvent and you can pull any color you want out of the magazine. Then rub it over a stencil and then you have a star or heart of whatever color you chose to use. Pretty cool trick right. I even traced different patterns onto my cards and colored them this way.

So I said all this to show you that you can accomplish what ever you set your mind to. Now lets set are minds to creating these heartfelt colorful creations that are loved ones will love and appreciate. Do not ever let someone tell you can't and, when you try to think outside of the box they are trying to put you in then you can humbly show them you can do it!

Chapter 1

Materials

Things you will need to make your heartfelt colorful creations and where to find them if you are incarcerated.

1. Drawing Pad/ Card Stock
2. Glue
3. Ruler/Straight Edge
4. Pencil colors/ Markers/ Colors
5. Pencil? pens
6. Transfer Paper
7. Shaders/ Rags

I will now take you down the list one at a time and tell you how to find or supplement for each item.

We will start with the art pad. I use a common art pad that they usually sell on commissary. If you are at a facility that does not sell them on commissary then more likely than not you can have them sent in by a loved one. My mom gave me only $20.00 a month but I asked her to by my art pads instead of putting the money on my commissary account. I could make more selling cards then the $20.00 dollars would have provided me and it gave me the since that I was working for the money instead of getting a hand out. For those of you who that this is not an option don't get discouraged you can make your own. If you take several sheets of blank paper and glue them together you can make your own card stock and make it as thick as you want. Giving up is not an option.

Glue is a little trickier and not commonly sold on commissary not in Texas any way. So I have used several different things in place of Elmer's. The most common thing we use on the inside is toothpaste. I have also used in a pinch oatmeal. If you make the oatmeal a little runny the excess water off the oatmeal will be sticky as it dries it will hold the paper together. My favorite substitute is hard candy. I purchase mint sticks and fruit sticks off of commissary just to use as glue substitute. Moisten them a little and they get super sticky. They will definitely hold your cards together.

The straight edge is pretty simple to figure out Protractors or rulers are commonly sold in commissary, but if by chance they are not sold at the facility you are at then what I would use is the back of a legal pad also the the cover of a hard back book will work nicely. You can even mark them in inches if you want.

Pencils colors/ Markers/ Colors fortunately in Texas we are allowed to purchase pencil colors off of commissary as well as water colors. They are not the highest quality of pencil colors but they are water colors. I will share a little trick I used while using my pencil colors. I would dip them in hair grease or baby oil sometimes even lotion if that was all I had this will soften the colors making them easier to apply and blend together. If you don't have access to any type of colors once again don't worry that what I am here for and what sets this book apart from other books the tricks of the trade. You are about to learn how to make your own pallet of colors that when used, will make you look brilliant to those around you. I have been in this situation. So as you read in the introduction you can use a rag, deodorant, and a magazine to create any color you need or want. I actually used this method for about two years while I was in county jail. I was producing cards so colorful that I was woken up at 3am by the sergeant and two of his officers yelling at me to give him my markers and colors. Then he said I also want to know how you are getting them and who brought them in to my jail. I told him I didn't have any colors or markers. That I was using deodorant and a magazine to produce my colorful creations. He of course told me I was lying to him. He then made me get out my living area so that he could proceed to shake my house down searching for colors and markers. I told him he was wasting his time. An hour later he was fuming mad that he could not find any contraband or the colors he was searching for. So he asked again Mr.Garrett where are they at? To this I said sergeant let me show that I am not lying to you about using deodorant a rag and a magazine to make the colors I color my cards with. So he agreed to let me show him and when I did show him the process he was in awe. He even actually apologized to me for calling me a liar and tearing my housing area up. He couldn't believe I was making such beautiful cards this way. So it goes to show that if you think outside the box you can accomplish anything you might not have thought possible. So in this process of pulling colors out of a magazine first find the color you want. Then take a rag then wrap it around your finger then rub it over the deodorant. Next rub it on the color you want now you are ready to start coloring. I have taken my rag and deodorant and tried rubbing it on other colors besides just the ones in magazines and discovered all kinds of things you can get colors off of skittles, m&m's, different pastry packages, and cookie packages so be creative and try to find other sources of color. The only limitations are the ones we put on ourselves so do not limit yourself. You can also use a shader the same way. I still use this method to do all my background work.

Pencils and pens are sold in most facilities as well that I have been a visitor of. How ever in the same county jail that I was in that didn't have any types of colors also didn't have any pencils. So I would roll up newspaper to a fine point dampen it and allow the ink run to the tip let it dry then use it as a pencil then I would use the bottom of a shower shoe to erase with.

Transfer paper is not hard to get in fact I usually just take a pencil and rub it on the back of the design I want to transfer then when I trace the design it will leave a lite picture of the design onto the card front that is easily erasable if you have to erase it. You can also use carbon paper but this is not recommended as it won't erase if you have to erase it for some reason. It is also harder to color over. If you don't have either one of these you can also use newspaper which I personally prefer over carbon paper it is easily erasable and not as messy as carbon paper.

Shaders and rags are easy to make. For rags I use a piece of old t-shirt or use a piece of sheet. I have made shaders out of everything from paper to earplugs. If you take a sheet of paper or toilet paper and roll it up as tight as you can then dampen them tie it with thread then let it dry and sharpen one the ends with razor blade. Remember to think outside the box.

So these are the materials you are going to need to get started. You are now on your way to becoming a colorful card creator so you can amaze the ones you love with heartfelt colorful cards and keep your locker box full of zoo-zoos and wham-whams!!!!! I have also discovered it makes me feel better to support myself than to have to burden my loved ones asking for money it also gives me a since of self worth. It feels good to know that if I can be self sufficient in here. I can accomplish things in the free world when I do get out of here. Where before I didn't have any sense of self worth. Even th smallest positive accomplishment has given me a start to believe in myself and give me a better self esteem. Remember I can't never could so believe you can and I promise you if you put forth the effort you can accomplish anything you set your mind too.

Chapter 2

Bi-Fold Cards

These are the simplest of all the cards in this book to create.
You will start by pulling a sheet of paper from your art pad or
whatever you chose to use as card stock. standard art pad are 9"x12". Take your
card stock and turn it where the the 12" side is horizontal and the 9" side is vertical
then measure 4" from the right side . Then 4" from the left side mark each one of
these measurements they will be your fold lines. Then fold the paper on the first mark
towards the middle. Then repeat this to the other side folding on the fold lines towards
the middle.

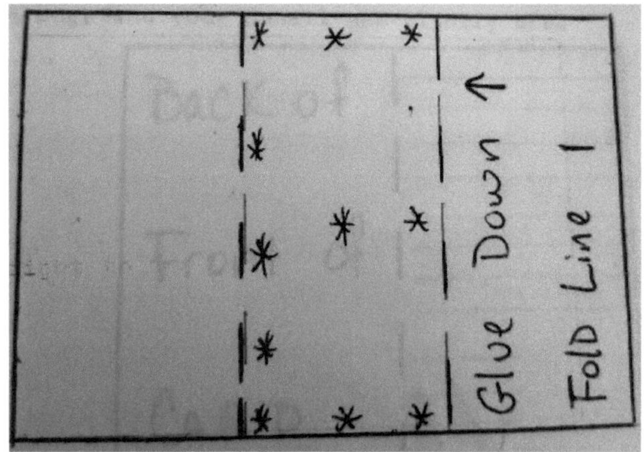

When You fold the second fold glue it
in the middle. you only have to use small
drops of glue so that it will dry quickly.
Look at the example to the right.(*=glue spots) I like to fold from the right to left and
glue this side down. Give it a few minutes to dry.

Then you will fold the other side over the middle. DO NOT I REPEAT DO NOT GLUE THISE SIDE DOWN!!!!!

This will be the front of your card.(see example below) The next step is to select the artwork you want to use for the card and

the poetry you will want to use for the inside if you chose to use a poem. I provided poems and artwork in the back of the book for you to use. Or you can write your own poetry writing is a good release and it means more when it comes from you. Know that no can convey what you want to say like you can. Okay lets get this colorful creation made.

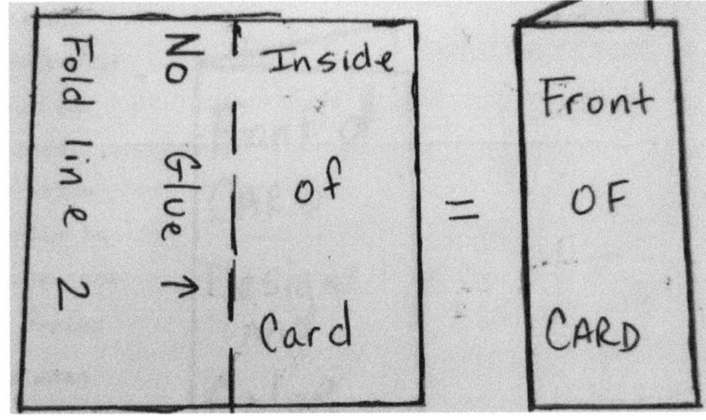

"I truly hope this book is everything you hoped it would be and the instructions are simple enough for you to understand and you are making beautiful card creations because of this book remember you can do anything you put your mind to"

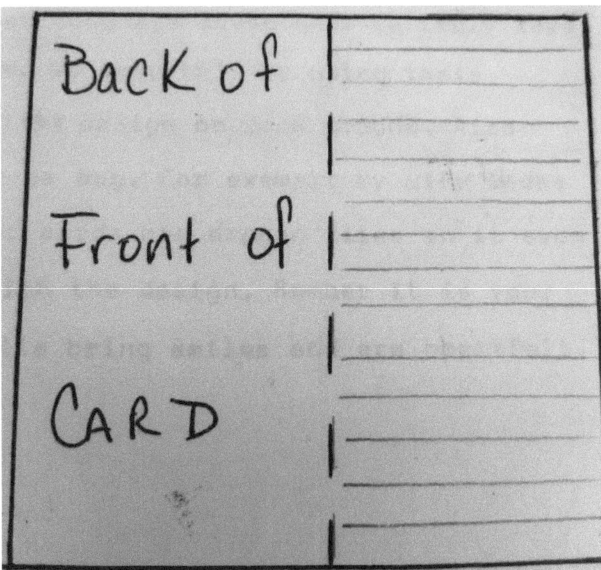

I usually start by putting the poem in first. Open the card to the side that is glued down to the middle. This is the inside of the card. Take your straight edge and your pencil and lightly draw lines on the inside of the card first. This will give you even lines to write the poem nice and straight. give the ink a minute to dry, and now you will want to erase the pencil lines.

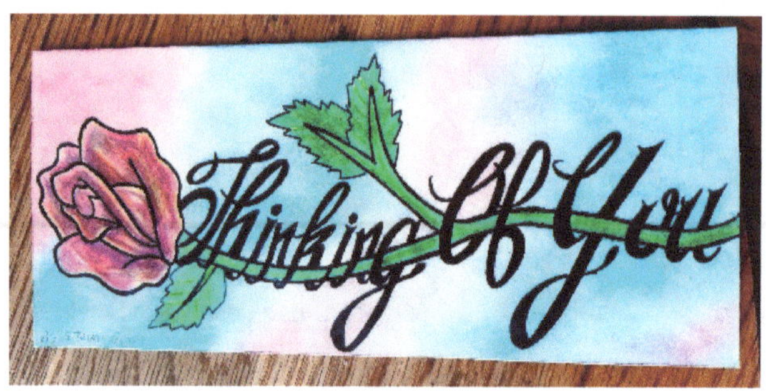

This is a sample of one of my colorful creations. Yours is gong to turn out just as nice when your finished!!!! I promise you are going to have your loved ones teared up and you locker box filled up before you know it

Now close the card back to the front and get ready to put the design on to your card. Before you trace the design on the front of the card place a piece of paper in the middle of the card so it won't leave an impression of your design on to the poem. Also when I select a design I want to use a separate sheet of paper and transfer the pattern to this paper first so you do not have to tear the design out of your book. You are almost finished with your first colorful creation. Now it is time to color your design. Always remember this is art make it yours there is no wrong way to do art. Be creative use your imagination!!

It is always the details that show are loved ones we truly love them and pay attention to them. We show this by using their favorite colors when coloring the design or back ground. Also details like a favorite flower or bug. For example my wife loves dragon flies. So everyone of her cards is going to have dragon flies in

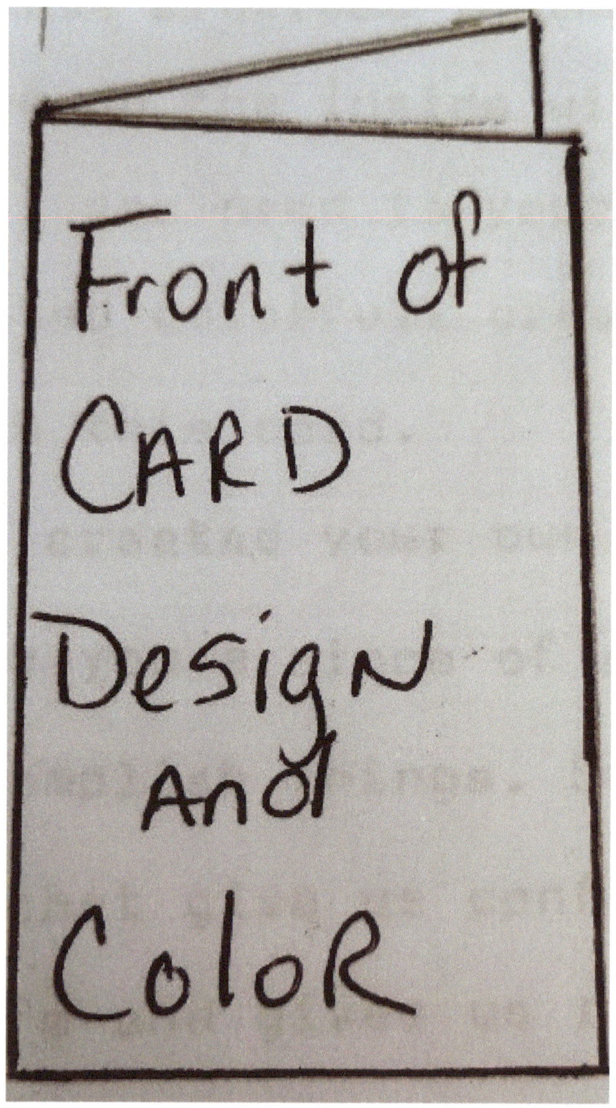

it. Even if they don't match the design of the card. Remember it is your creation and these little details bring smiles and are heartfelt. Nothing is better than when I send a card to a loved one and they told me it brought a tear of joy.

So it also important to remember that if it is a card to write Happy Birthday some where on the front. The poem will also express this to your loved ones. Now all you need to finish this card is the background and you will have your first colorful creation. See the chapter on backgrounds to finish your card.

Congratulations you just created your own colorful creation card. This should give you a since of accomplishment and confidence that you can accomplish things. Sometimes it is the small things we do in life that give us confidence to conquer the bigger things in life and give us reason to believe in ourselves. Showing us that we do have something to offer the world!!!!

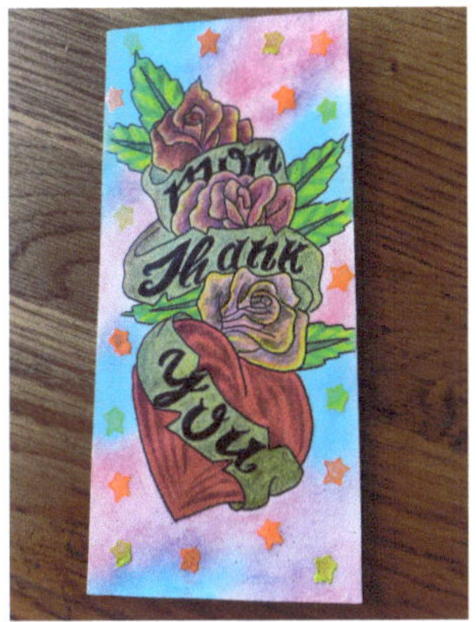

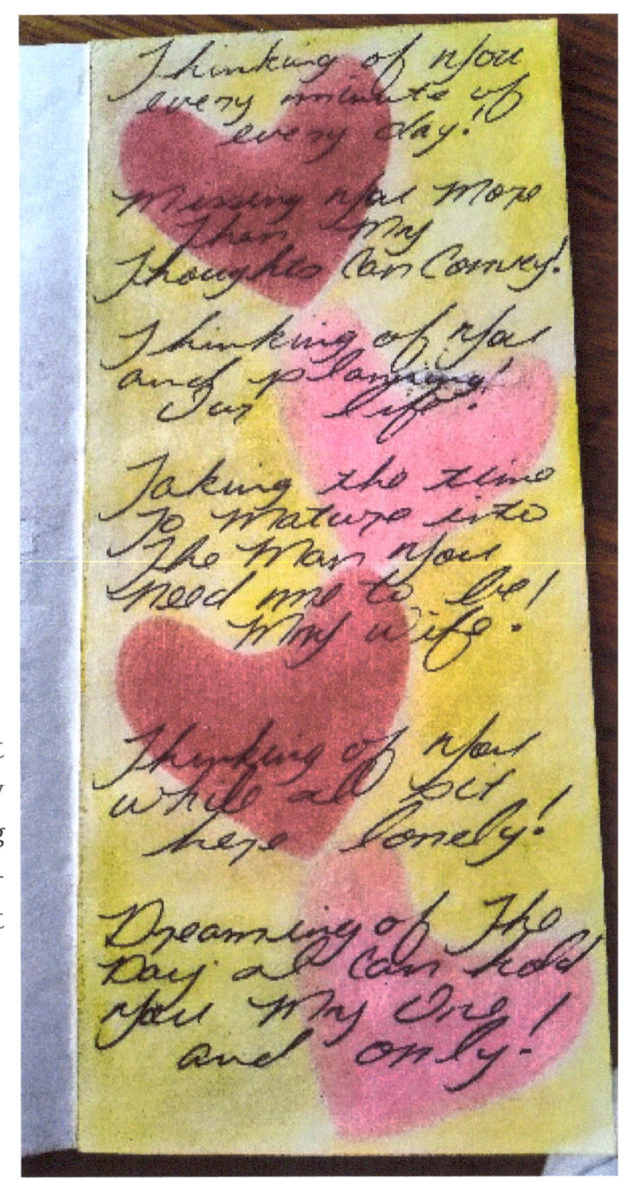

This is a sample of the inside and out of a completed bi-fold card I did for my Mother. Remember I have been making cards for twenty years so don't get discouraged if things don't come out perfect the first time practice makes perfect.

Chapter 3

Tri-Fold Cards

This card is just like the Bi-Fold card pretty much without having to glue any-thing down. It is a very simple card to create. It is exactly like the Bi-Fold card except you do not glue the first fold down like you do on Bi-Fold card.

So lets get started take a sheet of your art pad or what you will use for card stock. I will give you you the dimensions for the standard art pad because that is what I am using. If you are using something different just divide your card stock into

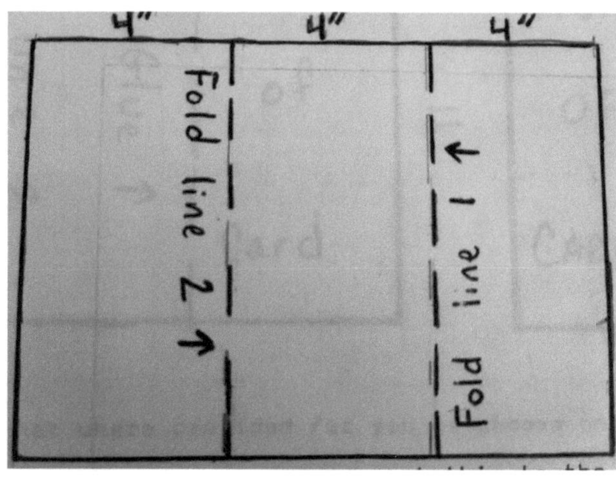

three even sections. The standard art pad is 9"x12". Turn your paper where the 12" side is horizontal. Then measure 4" from the right leave a mark. This will be your first fold line. From that mark measure 4"again and this will be your second fold line. On the first fold line fold from the outside towards the middle. Then repeat this process on the other side overlapping the first fold.

" Thankyou for taking time out of your life to learn to create these colorful
   creations with me. I truly pray that this book is informative and helpful!"

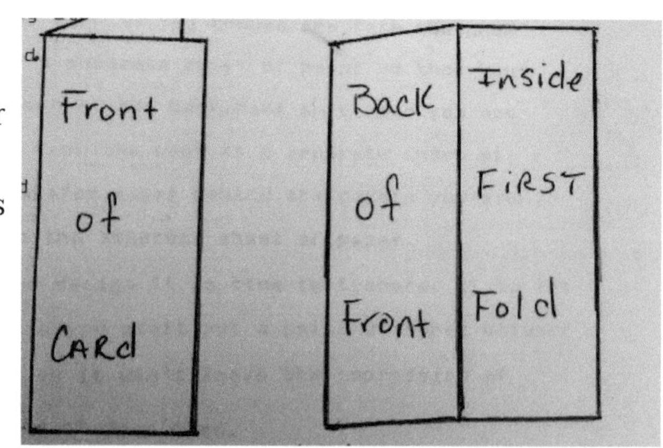

So now you are looking at the front of your card. It is now time to select a design for your card. You also need to decide what you you are going to put on the inside first fold this is where your poetry will go I like to add poetry here but you can also add more art if you chose. If you decide to add a poem lightly draw lines with your pencil. So that you can erase the lines when you finish writing your poem.

Now open up the tri-fold and get ready to write your letter on the inside of your card. Take your pencil and straight edge and draw light lines lightly across the entire card so that you can erase them once you write your letter. I always do all the writing I am going to do in the whole card before I add any artwork.

So basically I work from the inside out starting with letter. Then I add the poetry. You can find poems in the poetry section I provided for you or you can write your own. Once you get the letter and the poem erase the pencil lines. Now it is time to decorate the front of your card. Select some card art from the back or a design of your own. If you chose one from the back of the book transfer the picture to a separate sheet of paper so that you don't 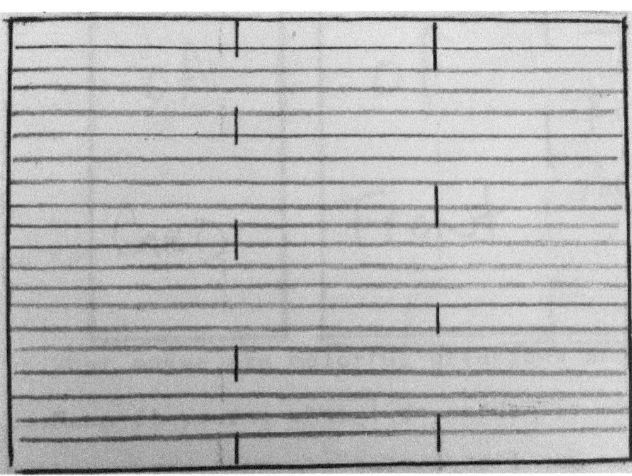 have to tear it out of the book. Make sure when you are transferring the pattern you place the paper you are transferring goes behind the picture then the transfer paper on the paper you are transferring to with the pencil or carbon facing the paper you are transferring to. If you put the carbon paper on the bottom still facing the paper you are transferring to you still get the image just backwards.

Now that you have chosen your art it is time to transfer it to the front of your card. Before you start put a piece of paper between the back of front and first inside fold where your poem is. You do this so that it won't leave the design impression on the inside of your card. 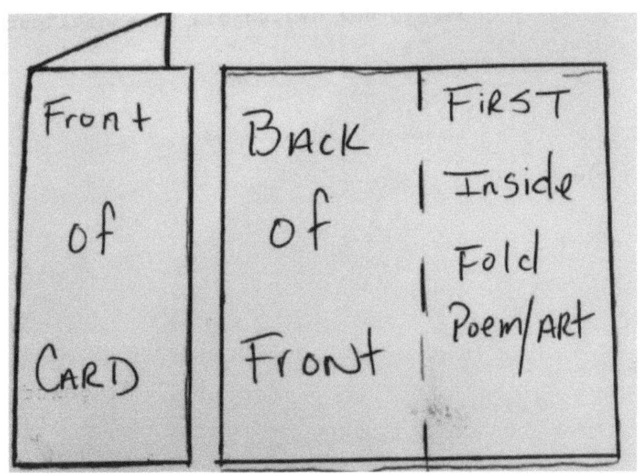

Now transfer your design to the front of your card. Once you get the design on the front before you color your design add any writing you want on the front your card. I like to do any writing before I do any coloring because pens do not write over the top of any type of coloring usually especially the colors you pull out of magazines. It is now time to bring your card to life and add color to it. What makes are colorful creations one of a kind is the details. Make it yours. When I do cards for my loved ones I always add color schemes or flowers and little things like dragonflies, ladybugs, or butterflies. Even if the don't go with the pattern art is art there is no right or wrong way to do it. It is your no one can tell you how to do it. Remember when you are doing cards for someone else ask them what little details they want in there card personalize it for them. this will bring you repeat customers. This is what will set us apart in custom cards business. Okay now you need to add your background see the background section to finish this card

I want you to take the time to reflect on the little things in life such as making this card or that you love someone enough to take the time to make them smile making them a card. It may not seem like much, but all the little things are what make the big things worth living for. Once we know we can complete the little things we gain confidence to accomplish the bigger things in life!!!!!

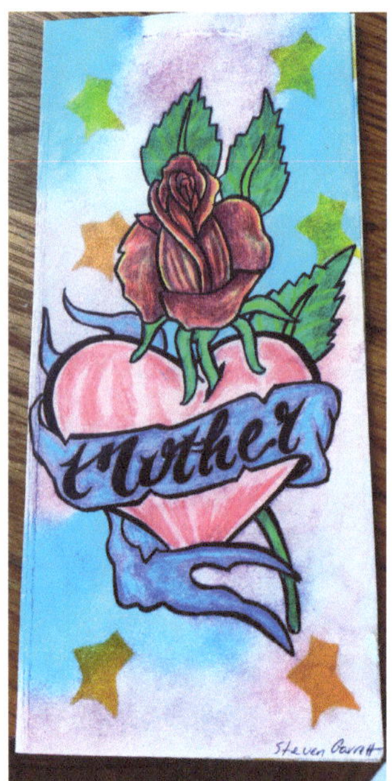

These are some samples of a finished tri-fold card I did for my mother. Remember I have been doing these cards for 20 years so I have lots of experience and it took several tries before my cards came out so nice. DON'T GIVE UP!!

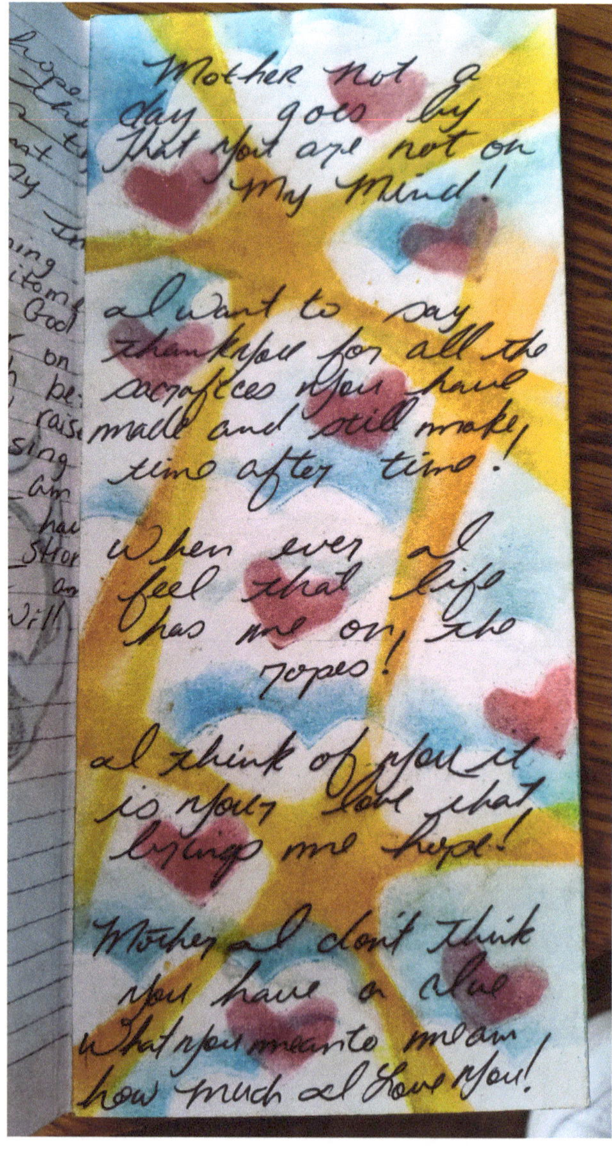

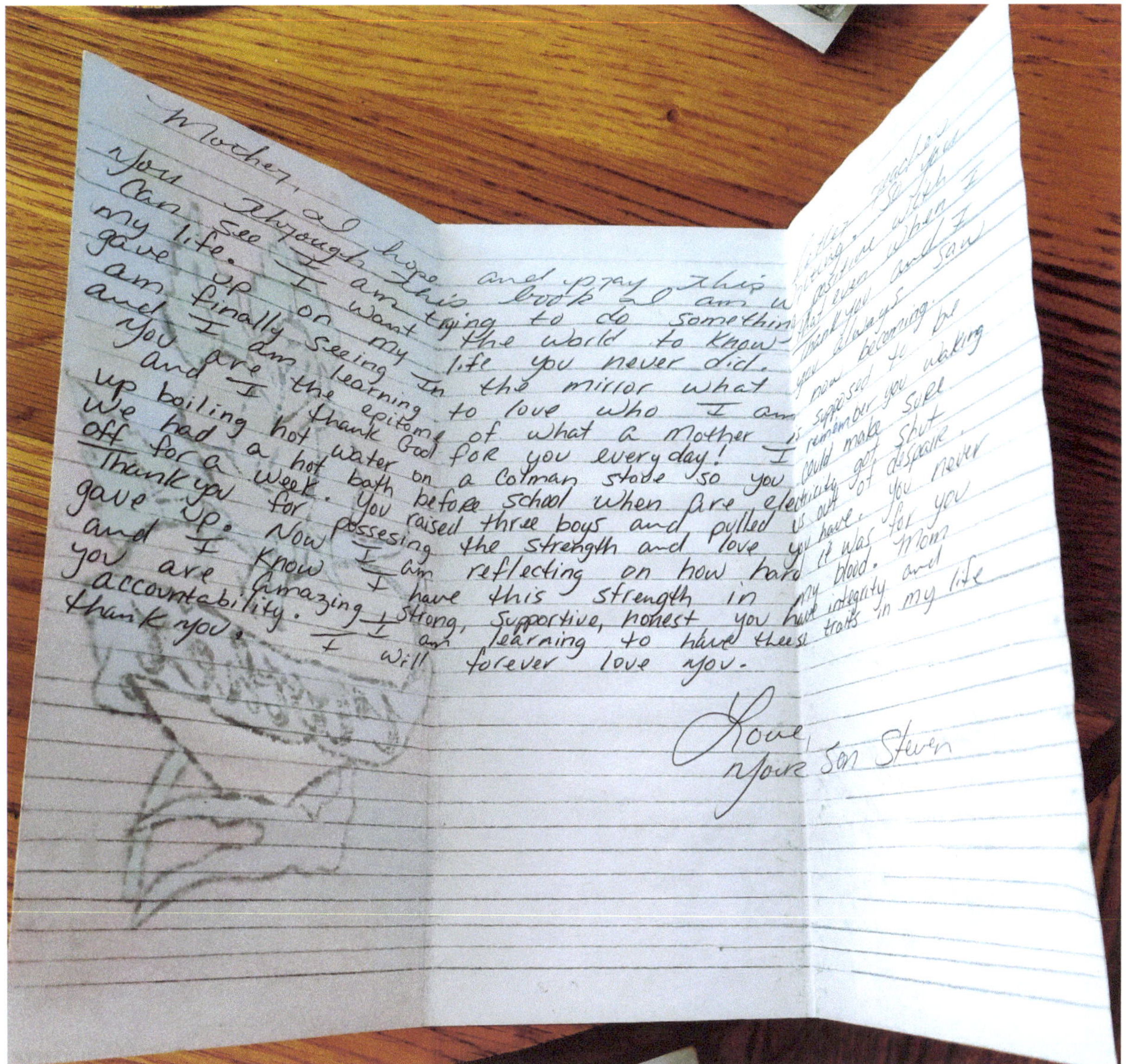

A CONVICTED HEART :By STEVEN GARRETT

As I sit here and reflect on my life there is a lot of hate , shame, turmoil and despair! Most of it self inflicted but blaming others out of embarrassment and fear! Always blaming others for my problems while drowning in my struggles and strife! For years I believed I was just not meant to succeed and content to live a drug addicts life! The scheming, the stealing, the robbing, and pillaging until I ended up in prison time and time again! When I finally looked in the mirror what looked back at me was my worst friend! The image looking back at me was truly begging for a change and that starts from within! I had to write everyone I loved that I stole from and lied to and admitted to everyone of those sins! IT was the hardest thing I ever did being honest to the ones I love telling them how I stole, lied, and denied but this is where I had to start! Now I am maturing into a man that has integrity and accountability now I am telling you the story of a convicted heart!!!!!

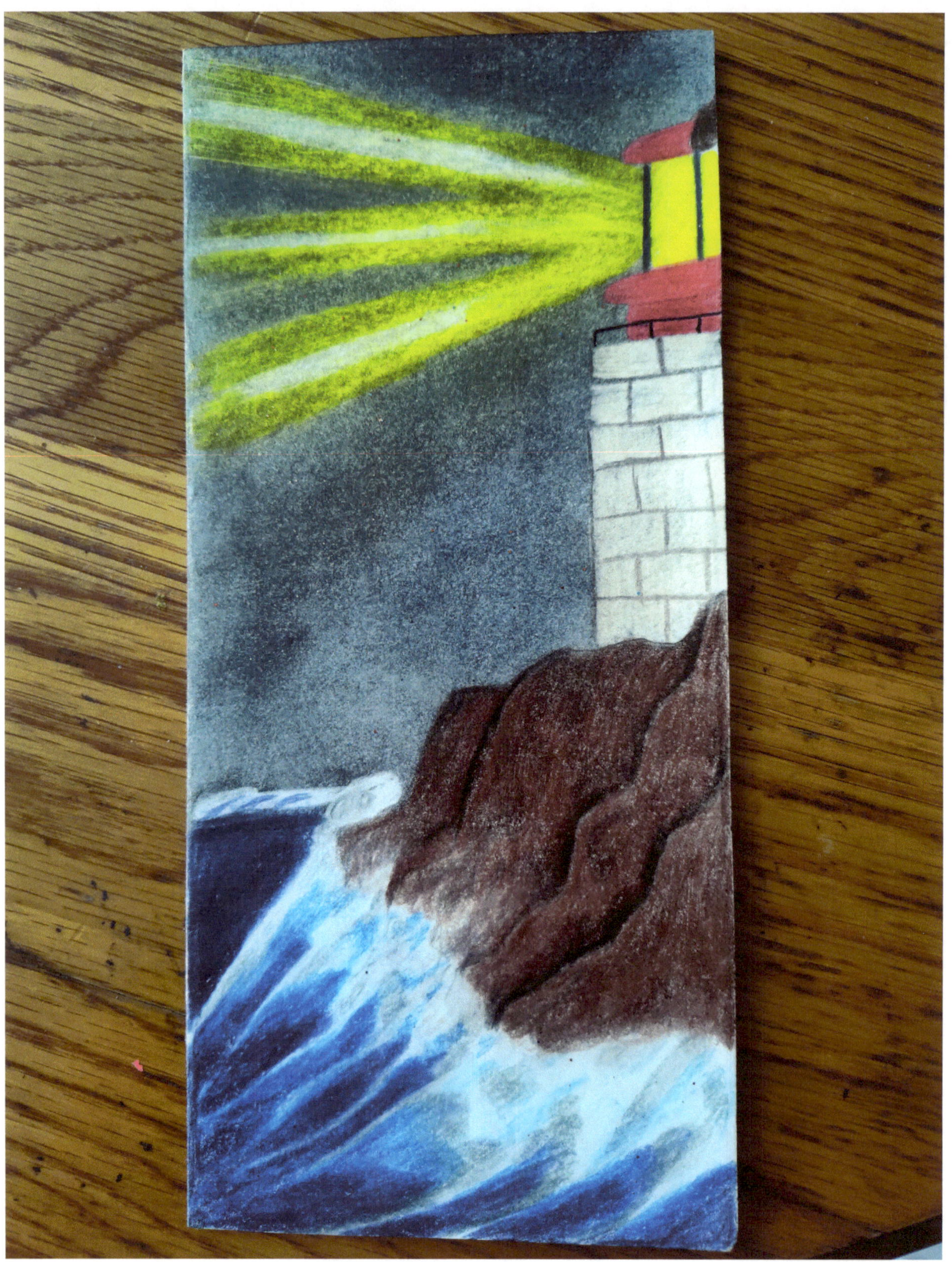

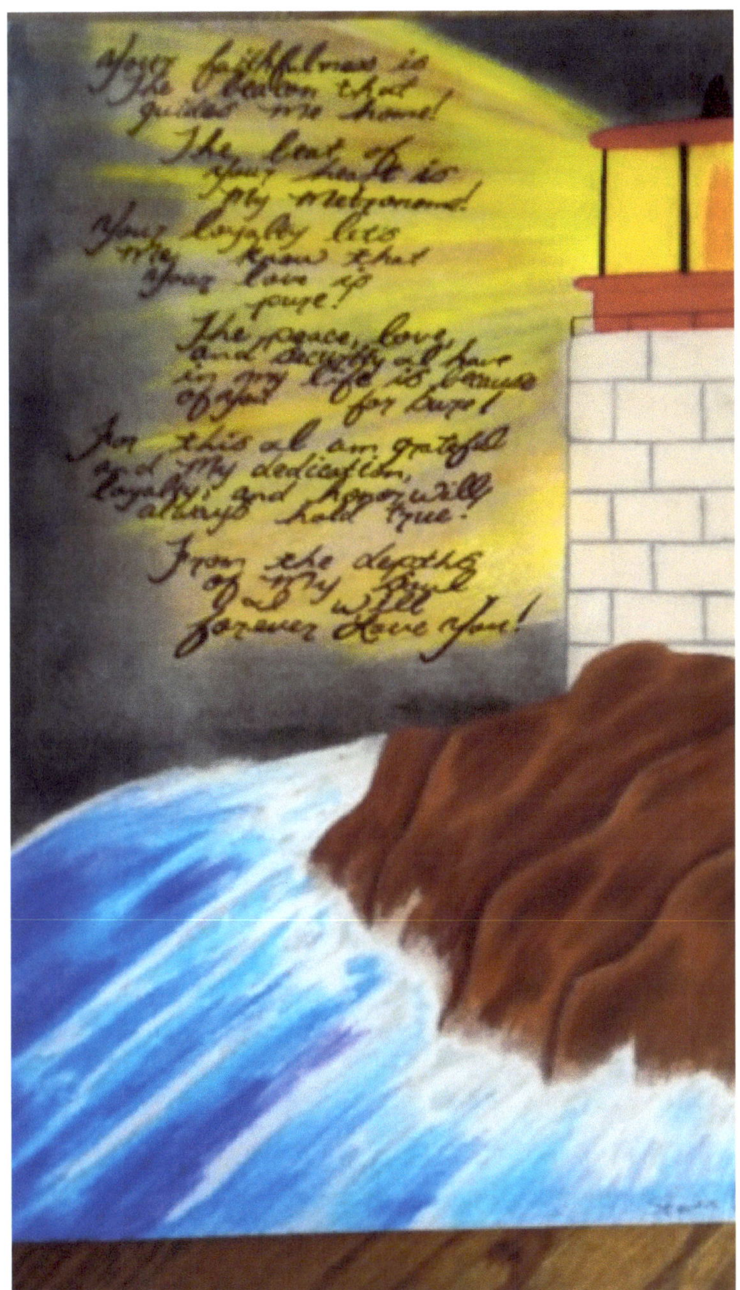

Chapter 4

Pop Out Card
Non-Traditional

In this chapter you will learn how to make pop-out cards. there is three pop-out cards of different degrees of difficulty that we will tackle.

Trust when I tell you that they are not so hard that you will be able to make these cards don't get discouraged you got this!!!!!!! These cards are a little challenging but fun and once you complete them you will be proud. They are guaranteed to get a smile and very often a tear by the recipient of the card. Okay lets get started. The first one we will tackle is the simplest of the three pop-outs. Take a sheet of paper out of your art pad and then just like the

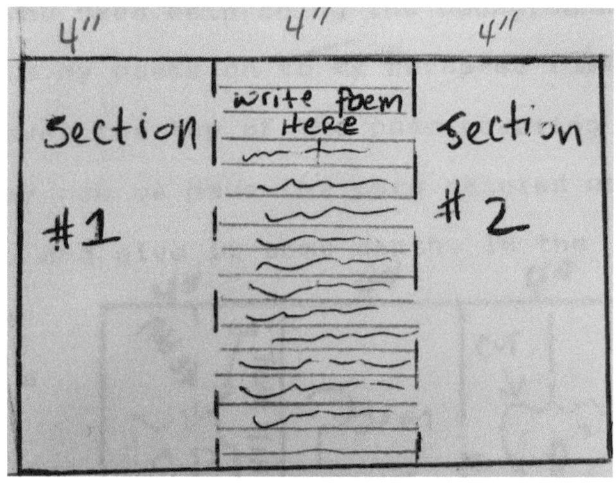

bi-fold card and tri-fold cards put the 12" side horizontal. Then measure your paper or card stock into three equal parts. I use typical 12"x 9" art pad so look at sample to the right and see how the set up should look like. So the dotted lines are going to be your fold lines if you mark this line do it lightly so you can erase the marks. Then in the center piece lightly draw lines like notebook paper so that when you add your poem you can write evenly and straight. Now go to the poetry section or add your own. Now put the poem in the center and erase the lines

. The next step is to select the art design you are going to use on this card. Get the design from the artwork chapter of this book or use a design of your own. You are going to put art on both sides of the poem. Each section is 4"x9". I am going to explain how to make this card as if you chose the same design of owls that I am using in the samples. Okay look at the diagram and in section one of your card take some transfer paper and transfer the female owl with the locked heart. Center the pattern so that you have about 2" from the top and the bottom. Look at the next sample insert if you need a visual.

Now the next step is to put the male owl in on the other side of the poem in section 2. Once you have the owls in place it is now time to color the owls. Use your imagination and remember to use favorite colors of the loved one you are going to send this to. Next it is time for the background. To do the the background go to the chapter on backgrounds for tips and ideas. I usually use black ink to write my poetry on to my cards so when applying the background I can apply it right over poem.

That way the complete card is covered in color. Be sure to look at the completed samples so you can get a visual if you need too. Okay now we have the card colored we are ready to make the card pop and give it some depth. In the first section where the female owl is measure 2" from the outside edge this is going to be fold line #3 this fold line is also going to be your cut line. The simplest way to find this cutline is to fold it just like the bi-fold card on the first fold line. Then fold the end back 2" then crease it. Then open the card back up and cut out the outline of everything on the inside of the crease to the poem. Then do the same thing on the other side with the male owl. Once you get both sides cut out

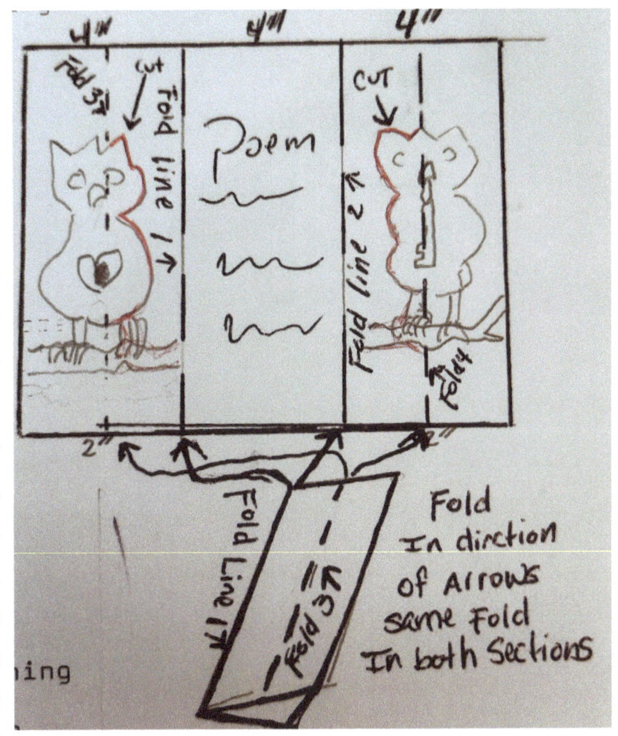

you will fold the card back on the crease/cutlines. See the finished examples of this card provide so can see exactly how this card should look when it is completed. This is probably my most popular card and the only pop-out card that doesn't require a bunch on of gluing. My wife always takes paper clips folds them in half and puts them on the bottom of the card like little legs. So that she can place the cards on the night stand and it will stand up with out falling down all time.

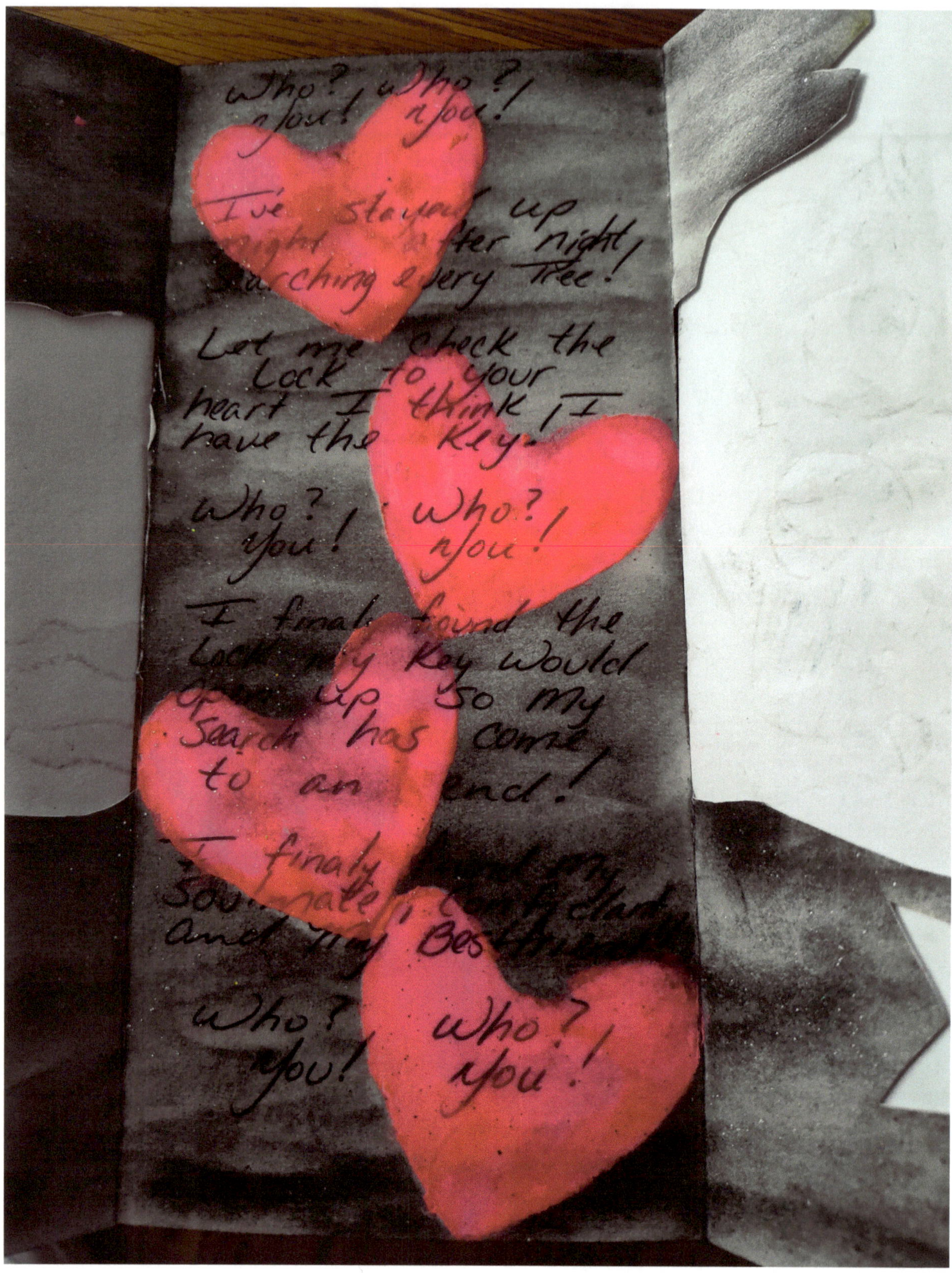
Who?! Who?!
You! You!

I've stayed up
night after night
searching every tree!

Let me check the
lock to your
heart I think I
have the key!

Who?! Who?!
You! You!

I finally found the
lock my key would
open up so my
search has come
to an end!

I finally found my
soulmate, best dad
and my best friend

Who?! Who?!
You! You!

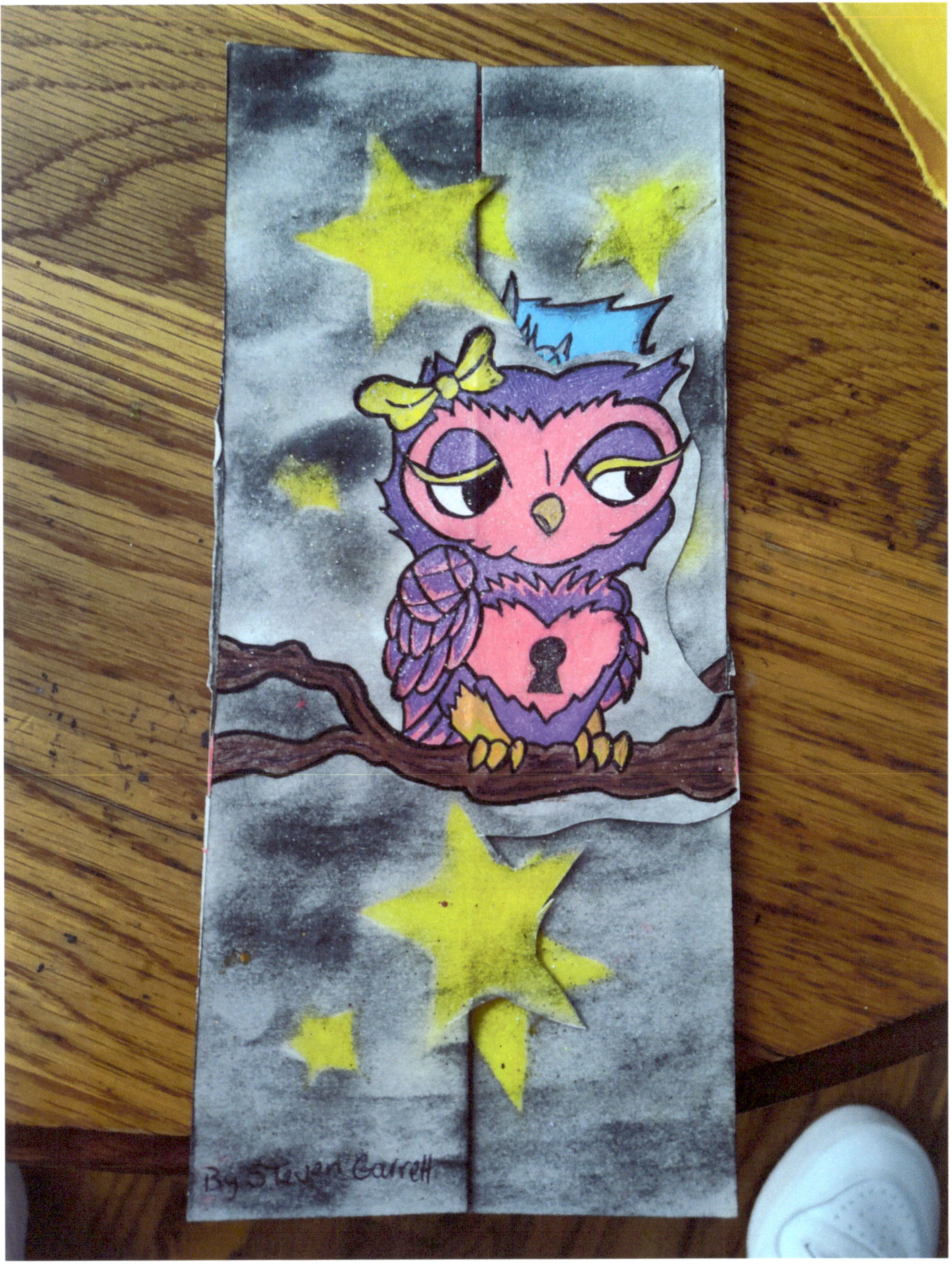
By Steven Garrett

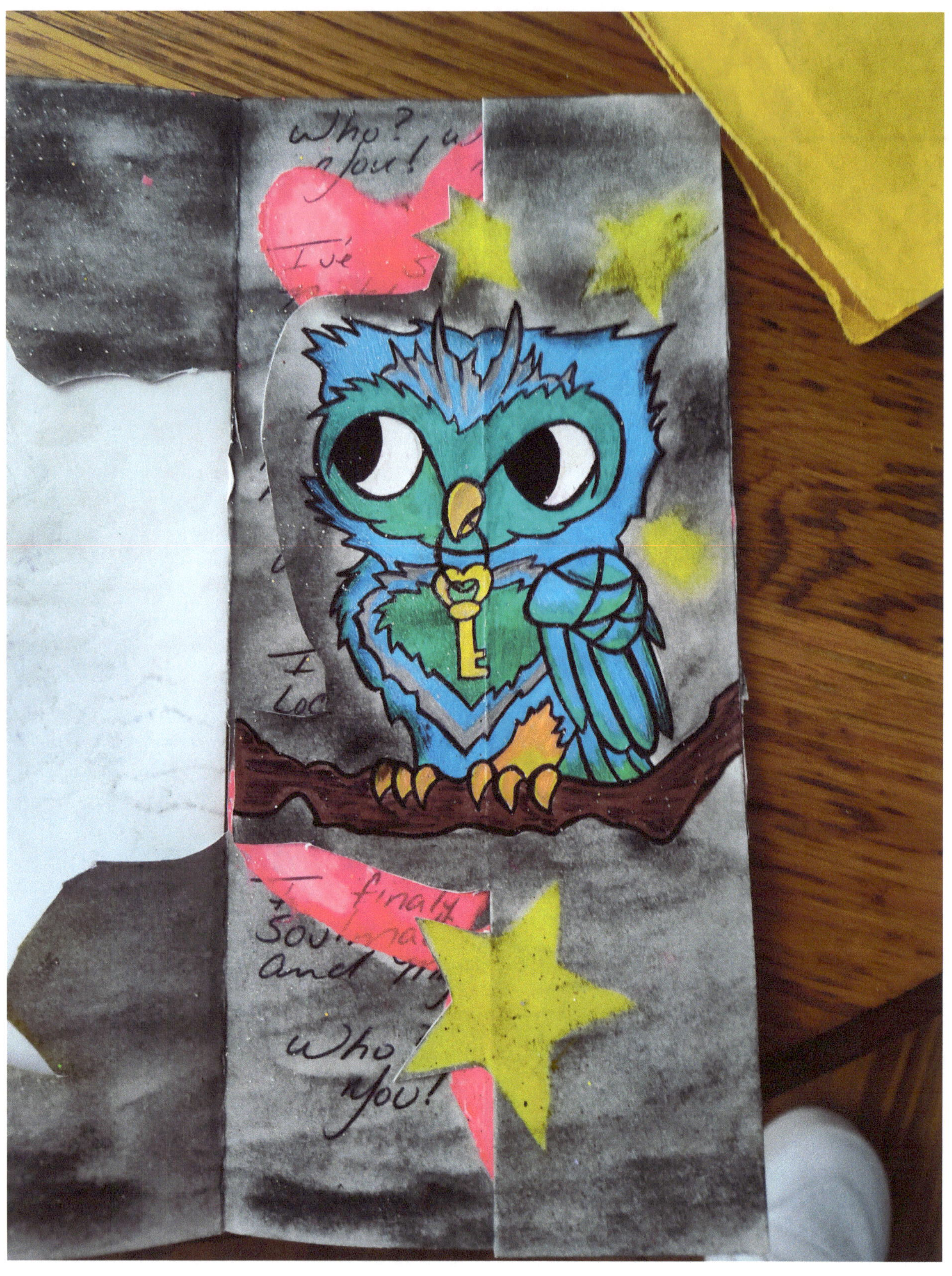

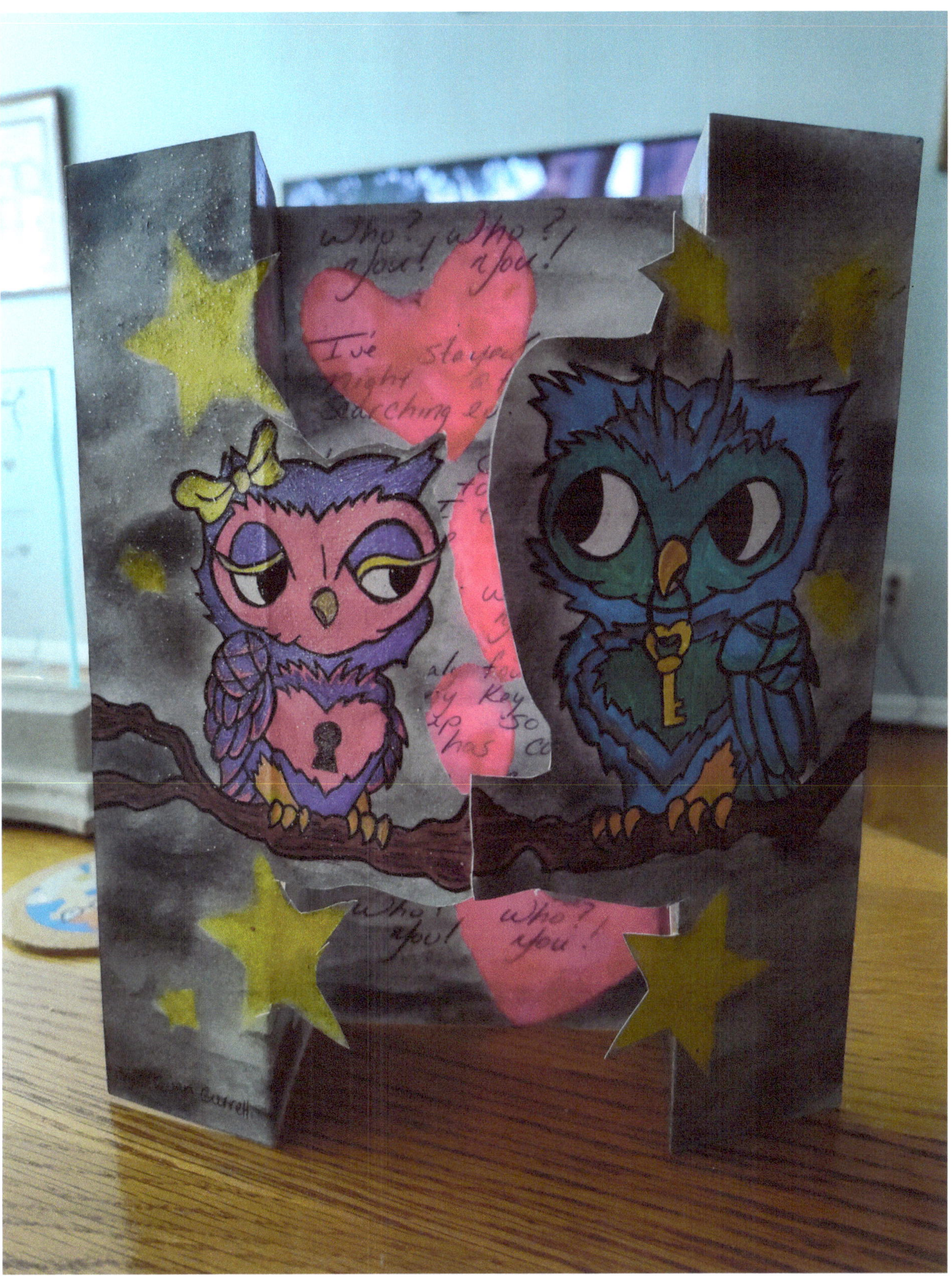
who?! who?!
you! you!
I've stayed
night
Searching ev
Key
so
has
who?
you!
who?!
you!!

Chapter 5

Pop-Out Card Traditional

The next pop-out card we will make is a more of a traditional style card that you will have to make an envelope for. You will learn how to make envelope in the stationary chapter. So lets get started this card is going to require two sheets of paper out of your art pad or card stock. The first thing you are going to do is take one of the sheets and fold it in half then open it back up.

Then on the fold line push the ends in towards the middle making triangular folds. Look at the insert to the right. Look at the finished sample at the end of the chapter see the roses that pop-out these are the triangular folds you are creating. Now set this part of the card to the side and get the other sheet of paper and fold it in the middle.

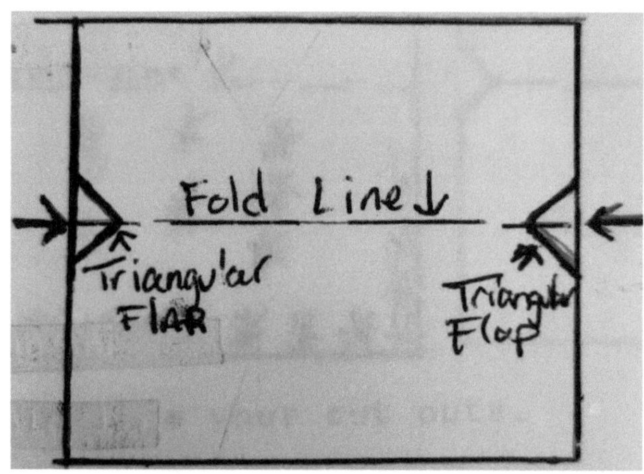

Turn it to where the fold is at the top and the card opens vertically.

This will be the front of the card. In the example I have used the front of the card says I love you in fancy script and the background is colored red. This is a simple front but very classy. You can chose any design you would like and get creative. Once you get the front colored complete the whole front design and background. You are now ready to complete the inside of the card.

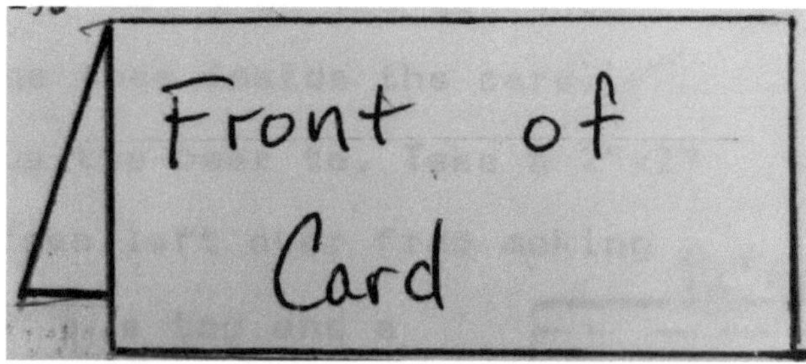

The inside of the card is going to be the piece of paper you put to the side with the triangular folds. You will see from the completed sample that on the half I am going to use for the bottom half I first came up with the quote I put in the inside of the card then colored it with several shades of green to resemble grass. Then stars and clouds for the top half of the card .Remember before you do any coloring you are going to do any writing you are going to do on inside first. Once you get the inside finished it is now time to begin to assemble the card.

The first thing you are going to do is glue the inside to the front. Open up the card to where the front is facing down and you are looking at a blank page and the colored front is facing the table. Make sure the colored half is at the top. Get your glue and follow the glue spots that are on the insert to the right. Make sour there is 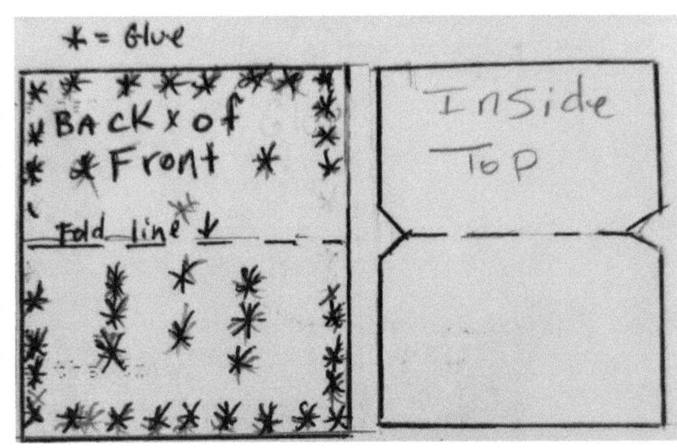

no glue where your triangular flaps are. Make sure when you glue inside page to the back of the front the top inside is on the colored part of the fronts back.

Now while this is drying we will make are cut outs that we will add that are going to pop out. You can see from the finished sample I made I chose A teddy bear holding a heart and some roses. Get another sheet of paper out of your art pad. Trace whatever pattern you want to use color them. These designs are going to be used to complete the pop-out part of your card. Once they are colored then cut them out and we will begin to assemble them to the card.

The first the thing we are going to do is make a to glue the bear to the card that will allow it to pop-out. Take 2"x2" piece of art pad I like tis little tab to have a little more support. So I will glue two pieces together. Just use left over pieces of art pad that you had from cutting out your cut outs. Fold it a 1/4" from the top and 1/4" from the bottom. Now fold it in the middle as well. Look at insert to the right. This is the tab you will use to glue the 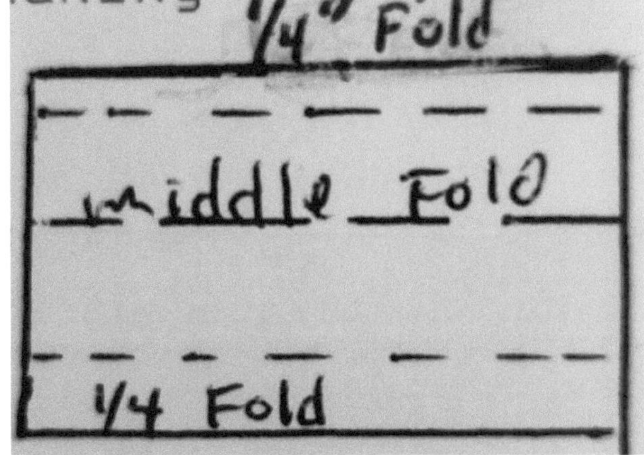

bear in place. You are going to line up the middle fold line with the middle fold line of the inside of the card. Then glue the 1/4" fold to the top half of the card. Allow this to dry and glue the other 1/4" fold to the bottom. Now once this dries then you will glue the bear to the tab on the bottom section. See completed sample. Then glue the roses to the triangular flaps. Make sure the roses are not going to stick out the side of card before you glue it down.

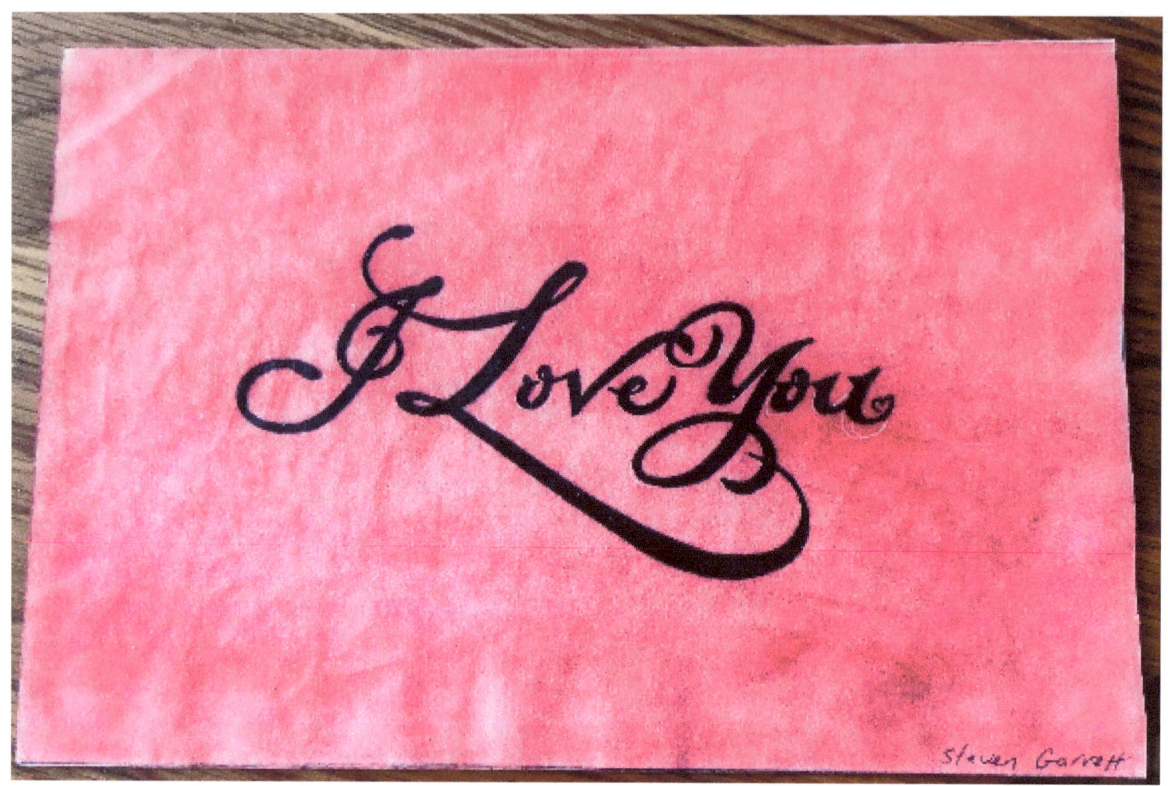

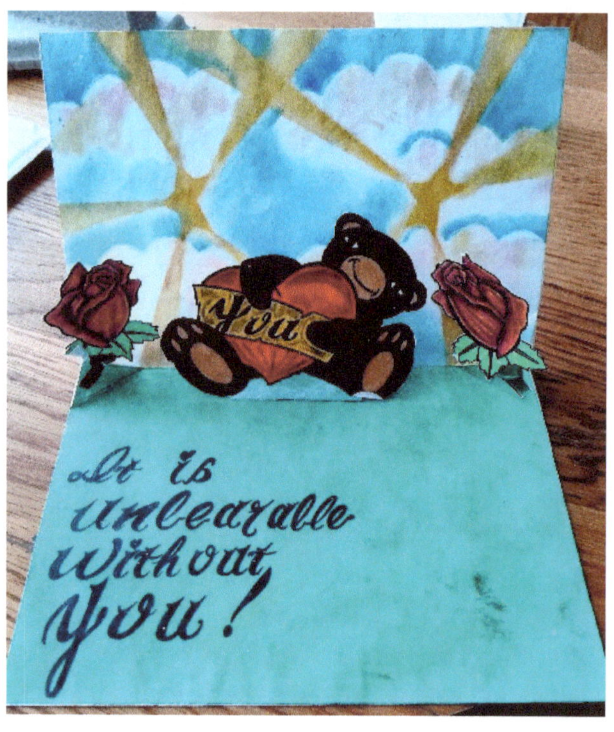

Chapter 6

Accordion Pop-Out Card

The third and final pop-out card is the accordion card this requires about four sheets of paper and about twice as much patience. When this card is finished it is by far the coolest of all the cards. Like I said it is a monster requiring a lot of work and patience, but worth every minute it takes to make. On your mark get set go and we are off to races!! Okay get the first sheet of paper fold it in half. Then get another one and fold it in half as well. One will be the front and inside back/top of the card.

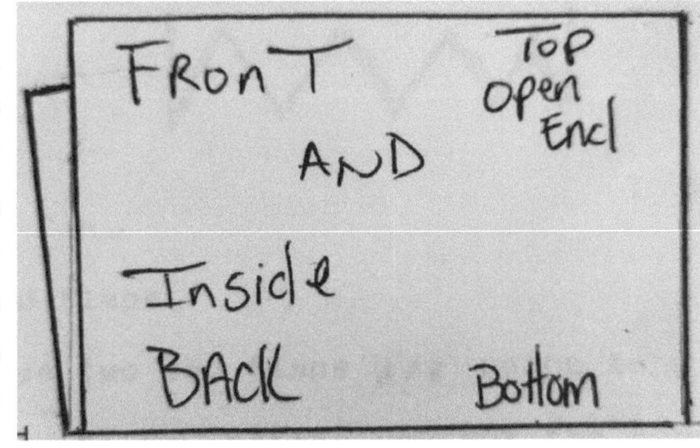

The other one will be the inside bottom and back of the card. The front will have the OPENED END AT THE TOP!!!!!!! For the finished sample you will see I chose to write the beginning of my greeting. After I did the writing I added two dragonflies and a sherbert haze background. Decorate the front any way you would like but keep in mind you are going to have a lot of artwork on the inside of the card. So it is a good idea to plan out the whole card before yo start this project. Go look at the finished examples at the end of the chapter. So you will have an idea of how you want to plan out your card. Now decorate the inside back/top. This where I put cupid and another part of my greeting. After you finish the front set it to the side and get the other piece you folded at the beginning. This will be the bottom inside and back of your card. Just like the front you want the open end at the top. This is where I chose to write the poem for my wife. I then decorated with hearts and the background was sherbert haze like the front. The next step will be to take another sheet of paper and transfer all the designs you are going to want to use on the inside. To glue to the accordion. I chose roses and a heart with an eternal flame. Color them and then go ahead and cut them out and set them to the side.

Okay We are getting there I hope you are still with me. Now get the fourth sheet of paper and color the whole sheet of paper whatever color you want your accordion to be. I chose green to represent grass. You are going to have to make sure the artwork you decide to use on the accordion is not taller than the card.

You will not want the artwork to stick out of the top or the sides when you close the card. Okay now we will make the accordion section of the card. Take the colored sheet of paper for the accordion

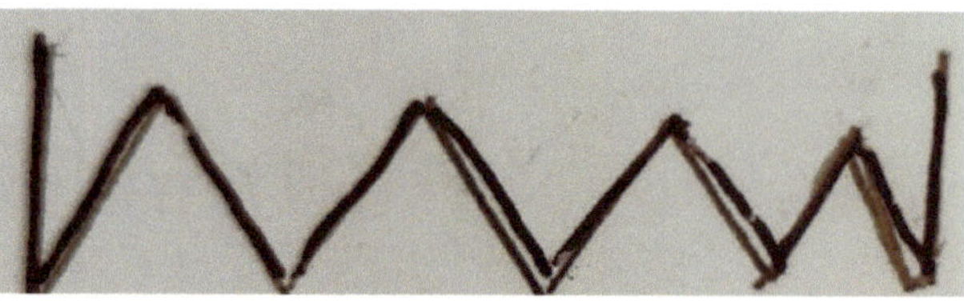

and fold it like you were making a paper fan. When you finish folding it make sure the two end flaps are facing the same direction. These flaps are going to be where you glue the front and back of your cards to. Now before you begin to put the card together make sure all your coloring and writing is done.

Okay everything is colored and all the cut outs are made. It is time to put it all together. Take the front and get the accordion. Then slide the first flap of the accordion into the opened end of the front. with the front facing away from the accordion. Then glue the whole front of the card together with the flap inside between the opened end you are making it all one piece. Then repeat this process with the last flap and the bottom/back of the card with the colored part facing the accordion

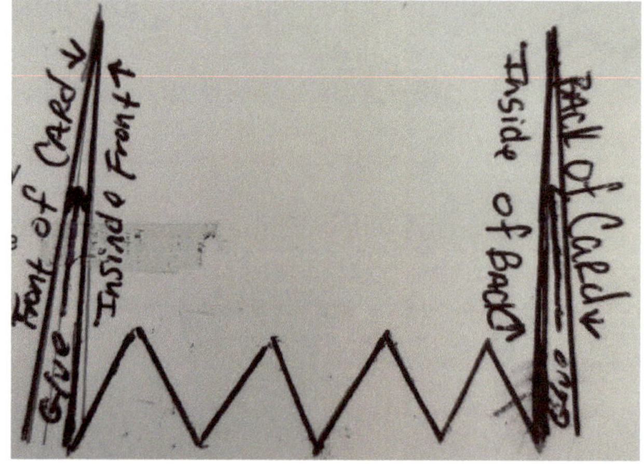

and the blank back side facing away from the accordion. Now that you have the accordion installed lets glue all the cut outs to the accordion. See the finished example I chose to use roses and the eternal flame heart. Now you a master card creator. When you send these home to your loved ones they are not going to believe you created them yourself.

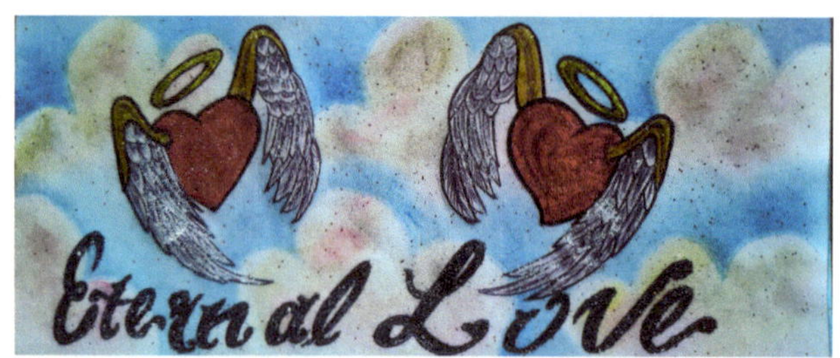

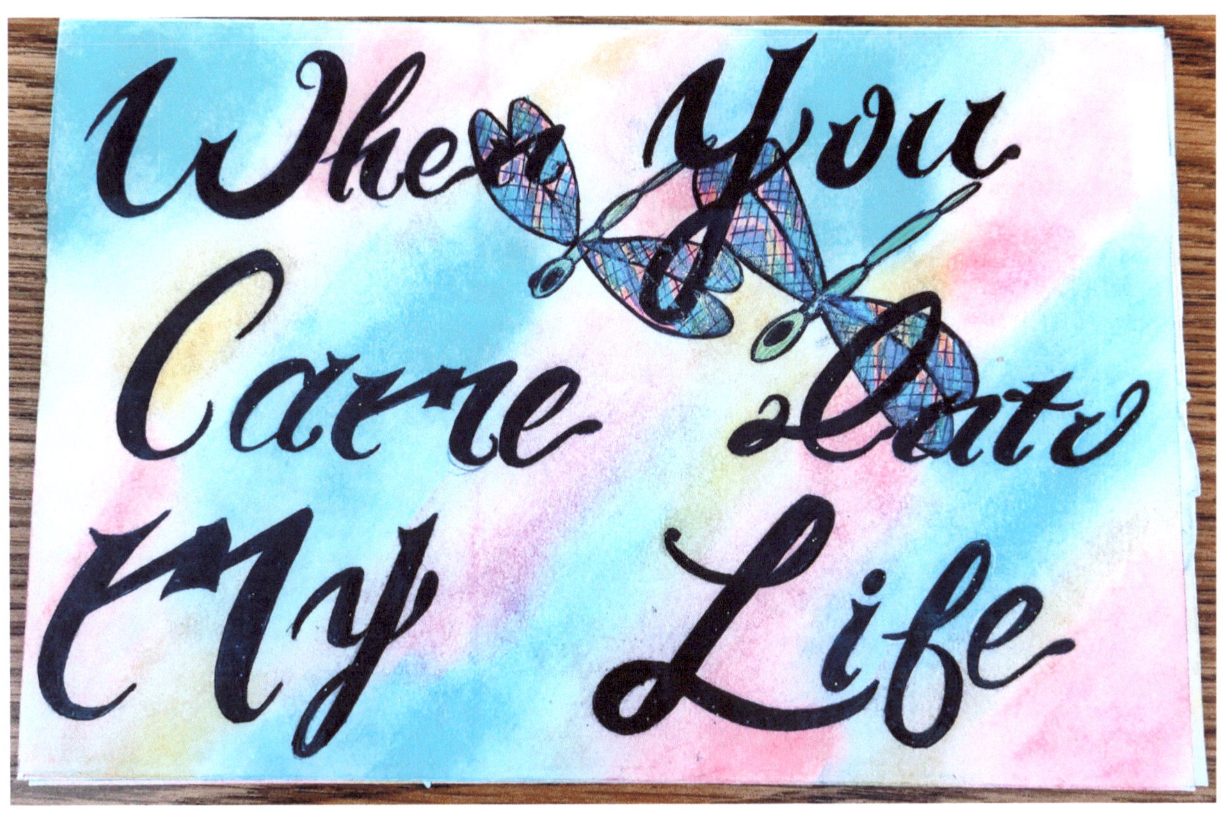

When You
Came Into
My Life

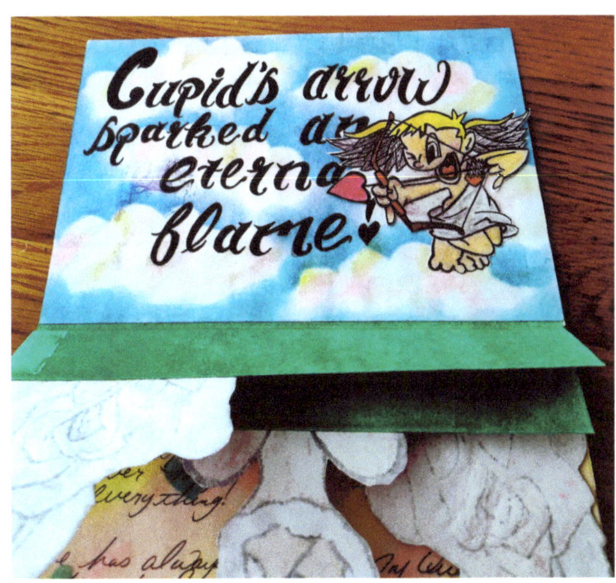

Cupid's arrow
sparked an
eterna
flame

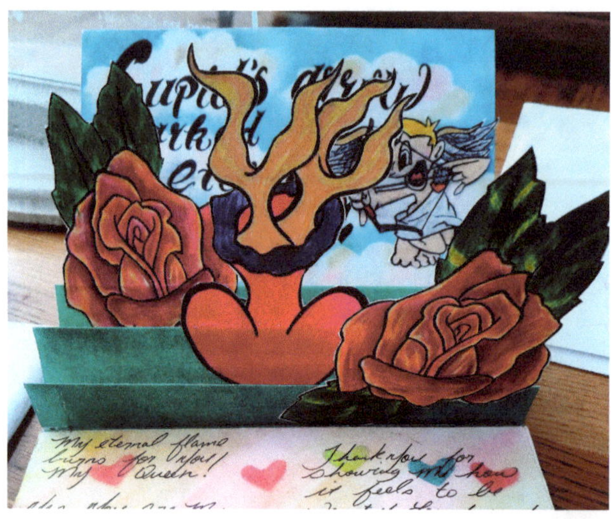

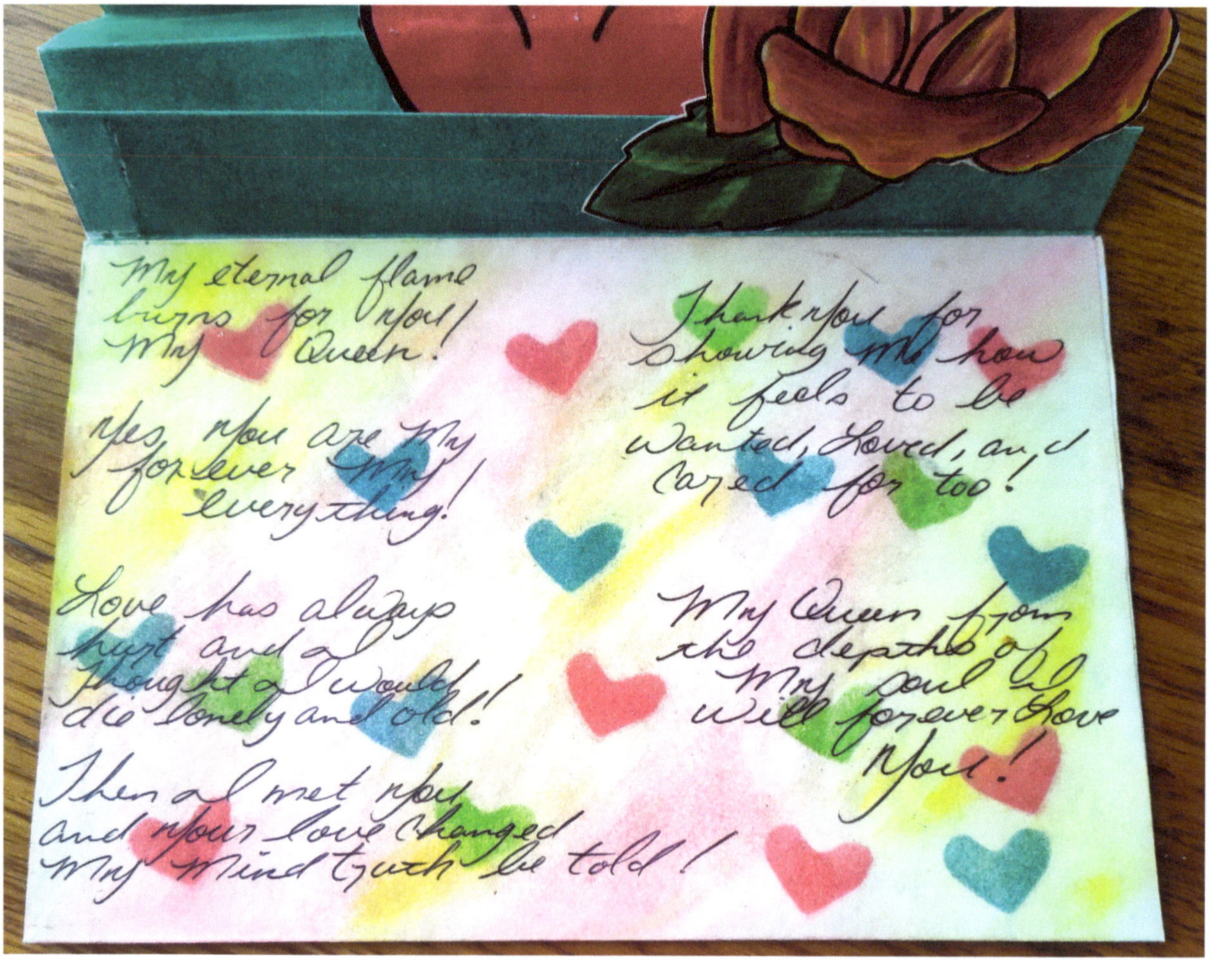

Chapter 7

3D/Puzzle Card

They say save the best for last. This card is fairly simple to create but it is really cool. First got to the art design section and find the 3D/puzzle card cut out. I chose to use the teddy bear but you can use the same design and turn it into whatever you want to. I have done this as a dinosaur, raccoon, puppy, and several other animals. Just be creative and use your imagination. What you will do is take a regular sheet of paper and transfer the cut out design to it. This way you don't have to tear your book up.

Once you have the pattern have the pattern then you have to find some sort of sturdy material to make your cut outs out of. What I use more often than not is the back of a legal pad or the back of your art pad. Trace the pattern on to this material and cut out all the pieces. Then take all the pieces and glue them to pieces of paper out of your art pad front and back. Make sure you lightly cover the whole cut out surface area with glue then apply the paper . Give them plenty of time to dry. Once they have dried cut them out and 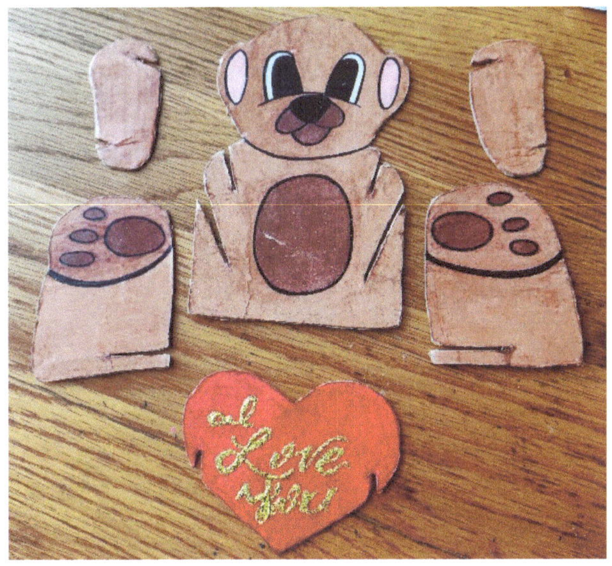 now you are going to color them. Draw the face and paws onto the pieces. The heart you will color it and put whatever you want into the heart. I usually write I love you in a nice font. Another thing I have done is use a picture and glue it to the heart and then trim it to the shape of the heart. Once you get all the pieces colored assemble the puzzle. You might have to trim it a little to get all put together right. Take a look at the completed example if you need a visual to help you assemble it. Sometimes you might have to give it extra support in some areas. I use little pieces of popsicle sticks or pieces of cut up pencil.

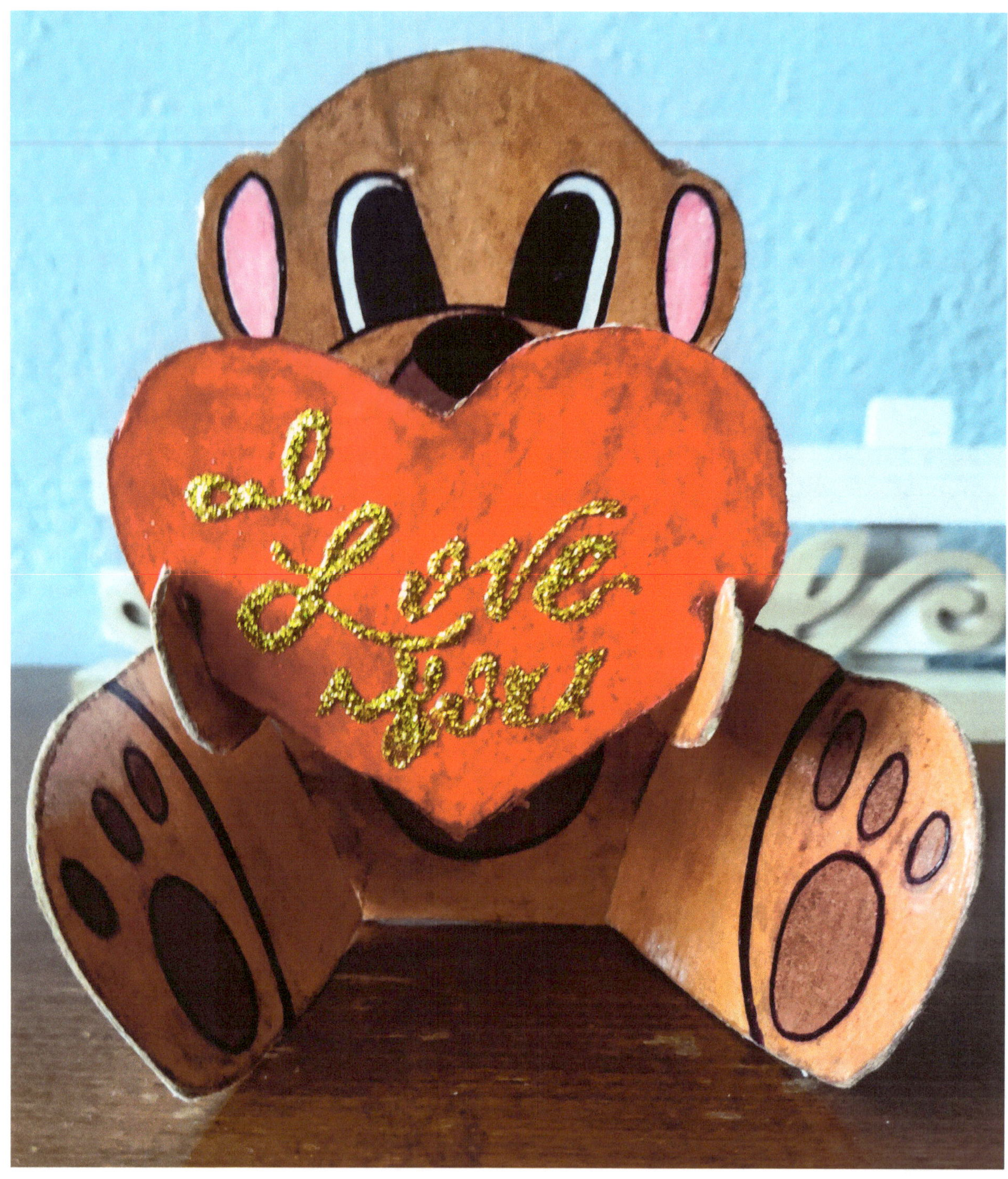
I Love You

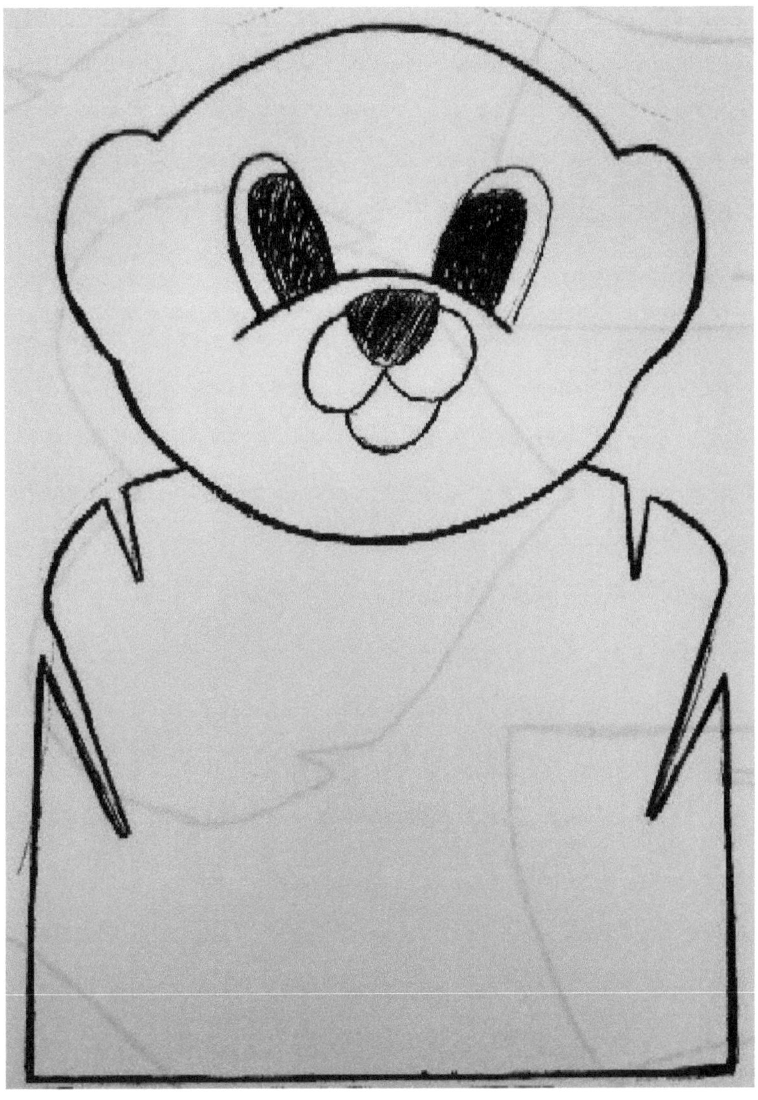

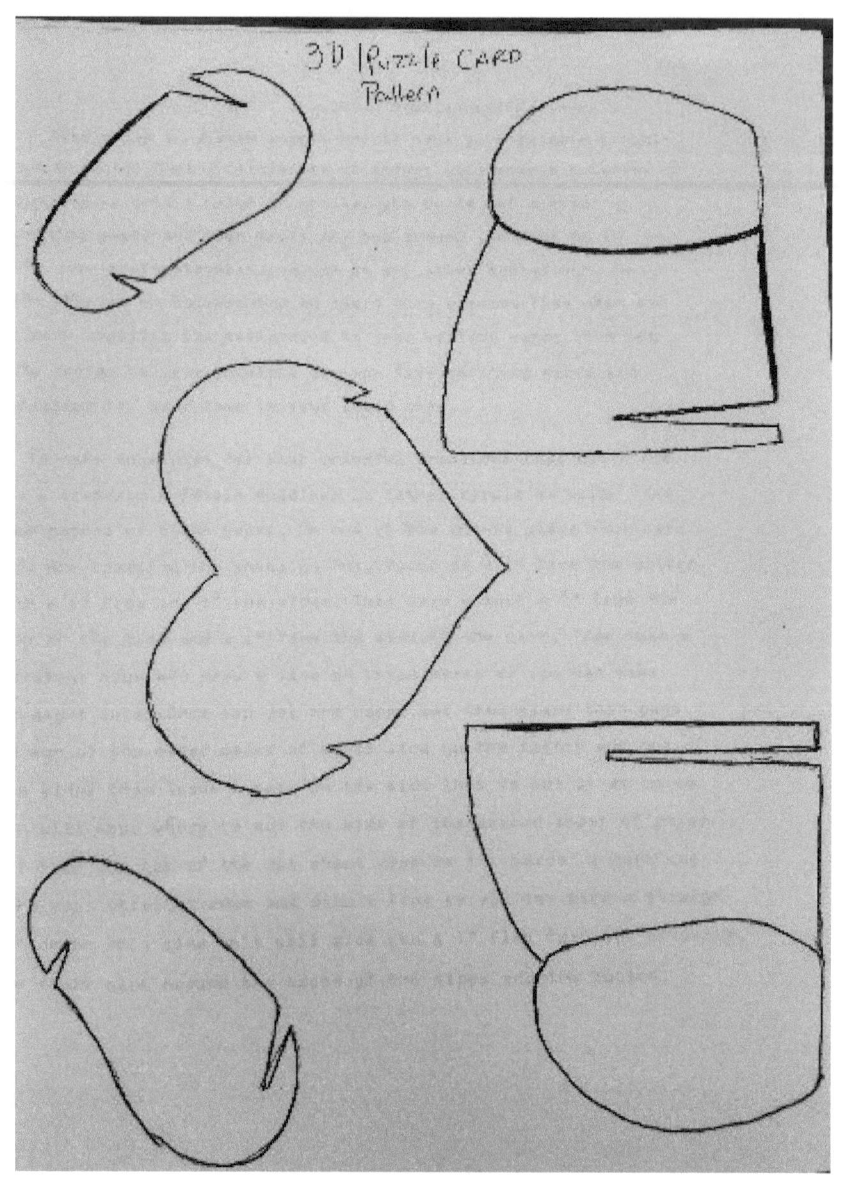
3D Puzzle Card
Pattern

<h1 style="text-align:center">Chapter 8</h1>

<h1 style="text-align:center">Stationary/Envelopes</h1>

Stationary is a very simple way to make your letters bright and colorful. Just a little bit of effort will change a letter into a piece of art. All you do is get a sheet of paper you would normally write your letter on. Then use the same stencils you use to do you backgrounds and put any background you want to your letter. Go to the background chapter to learn this process if you haven't done that yet. Then when you finish this process to the writing paper do the same process to an envelope. Now you have matching paper and envelope to send home to your loved ones.

To make envelopes for your colorful creations that don't fit in a standard business envelope is rather simple as well. Take two pieces of blank paper. On one of the sheets place your card a 1/4"from the bottom of the paper and a 1/4"from one of the sides of the paper then measure a 1/4" from the other side and from the top. Then take a straight edge and make a straight line on the mark you made for the top and the side. Cut the paper on these lines nice and straight. Once you cut the paper then place this on to the other piece paper with the edge's lined on one side and the bottom make a mark on the opposite side and cut the second piece of paper but leave the top to the second sheet this will be your flap. Now apply glue to the edges on three sides leaving the top unglued. Now you have an envelope if have to trim the top flap that is fine trim it to how you want it to close.

I usually sell 2 sheets of stationary and an envelope for $1.00and an envelope back. Just keep in mind you put the prices on your creations for what you feel your time and art is worth. I always try and look out for those who don't have much and stationary is a cheap way to bring a smile to someone. This will give you an amazing feeling of warmth in your soul to help those who need it. I always try to keep extra hygiene products to help people out with. There where a lot of times in life when I needed help and didn't always get it. I think this has made me an even more gracious giver and shows me my growth as a human being. It also seems the more I bless people the more blessings I receive. I used to be a greedy hateful schemer in life. Life always seemed to be so cut throat and not worth living. I went to program in prison called PEP or the prison entrepreneurship program. The very first thing they asked me to do was write on a sheet of paper that if I WERE TO DIE TODAY WHO WOULD WRITE MY EULOGY AND WHAT WOULD IT SAY!!! I started crying my instructor asked me what was wrong and I told him I wouldn't have anyone to come pick my body up much less write a eulogy. From that point right there I knew I didn't want to die like that. I knew I had to change every part of who I was as a person. I challenge you to answer this question and if you can look inside yourself to start the healing process. The place I had to start was writing everyone who loved that I did wrong and to own up to all the hurt and pain I caused. I got a letter back from my mother and put it on my desk not wanting to read it. I knew I had lost my mother admitting to all the stuff I had done. It took me five weeks of my cellmate telling me I need to read that letter. So I finally built up the courage to read it. When I finally opened it up all it said is I am writing this letter with my eye's full of tears not out hurt or pain but because I finally got my son back. So remember you may not be able to change the past. You do have the power to apologize. Once your feet start lining up with your mouth people will recognize and doors will start to open up.

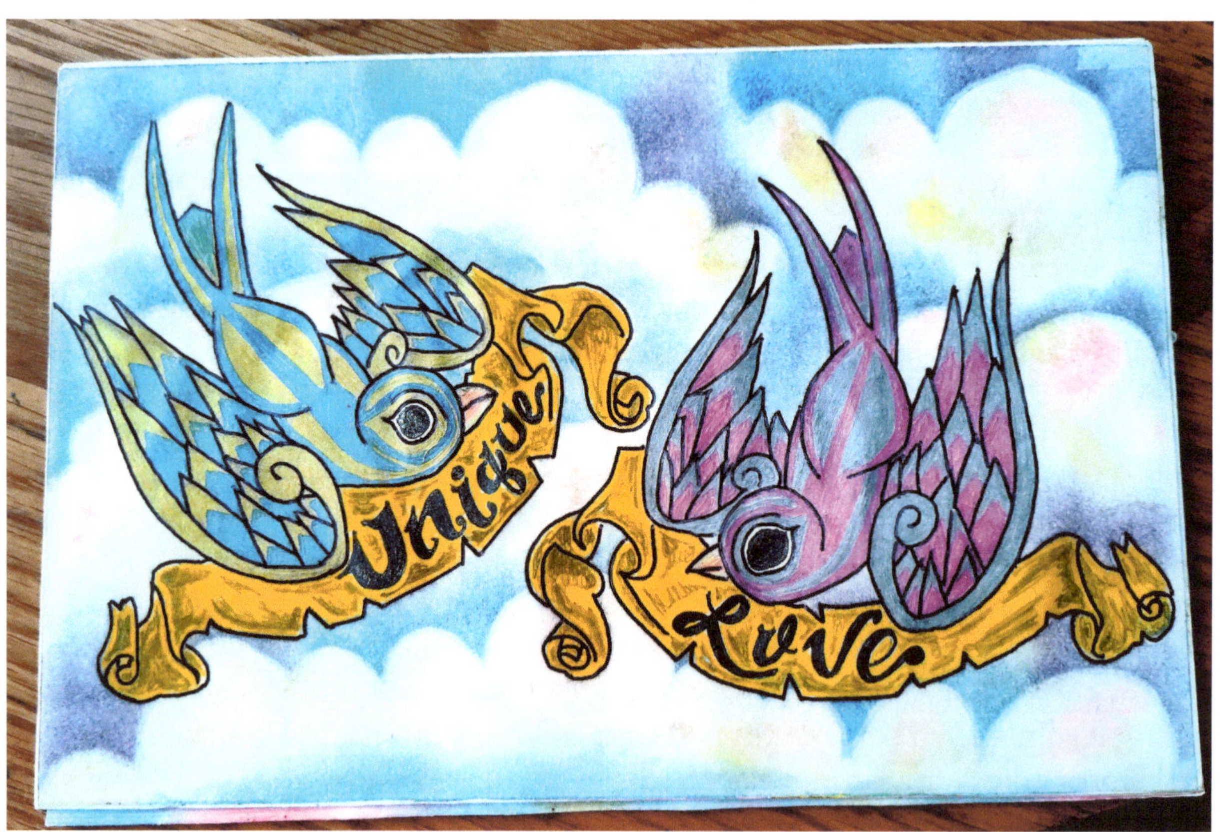

<h1 style="text-align:center">Chapter 9</h1>

<h1 style="text-align:center">Backgrounds</h1>

Backgrounds are always the final step in the coloring process of my colorful creations. They are also where I get the most creative in choosing color schemes. That are different than what nature has to offer.

This is where you can really think outside the box and just make purple grass or red clouds.

Basically whatever you want to do it is your creation. That is what I love about art there is no right or wrong. It is what you want and for every person who doesn't like what you put out there are ten more who will love it. I use my art as an escape from these walls. When I am creating cards or artwork for my loved ones or clients loved ones. It is an amazing feeling to give someone a smile. I consume my life now trying to bring joy to others. Sorry to get off track.

To start the process find a good rag a piece of sheet or old t-shirt works the best. I also get my deodorant and magazines for color. For those of you who don't have a clue what I am talking about I will describe this method of coloring again.

Okay what you will do is get your rag wrap it around around your finger. Rub it over the deodorant and then find any color you want in a magazine. The deodorant will act as a solvent and pull the color off the magazine on to your rag and now you are ready to color.

I have included stencils of clouds, hearts, stars, and other stencils I commonly use for my backgrounds. When I apply stars I like to at the points take a straight edge and apply color down the edge of the straight edge on all five points this will give it a starburst effect. You can see what I am talking about in some of the finished examples.

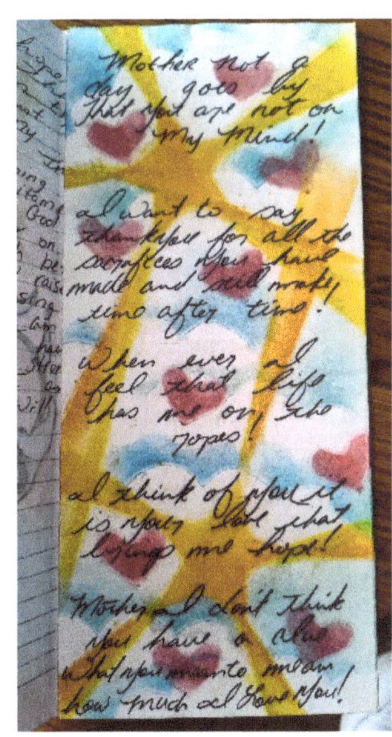

Then I will go and add clouds all around the stars using the stencils provided. After I put the clouds down I like to go add pink and yellow highlights in the clouds. Then on the insides of the cards I like to add hearts I put them right over the poem then color around the hearts. Always remember if get color where you don't want take your rag and put some deodorant on it and you can remove the color .

I always use my imagination in my backgrounds. I have made green clouds with blue grass. I like to find out favorite colors of the people I am making the cards for and personalize the card with them. Even if the colors are not natural. This lets them know you pay attention to them this brings joy and happiness. Love is in the details. You can tell someone you love them a million times, but when actions tell them that you love them they believe it and feel it. Actions always speak louder than words. Take your rag and deodorant and try taking colors off of other things than in magazines. I have gotten colors off pastry packages and a lot of other things if you see a color you want see if you can get it.

Take pride in anything you do because if it is worth doing. Then it is worth doing it to the best of your ability. Whether it making a greeting card or taking the trash out. Remember there is one thing you can never get back in life and that is time. Once it is gone it is gone for good. Time is are greatest asset it is free and yours to do what you want to do with it. So if anything is worth spending you greatest asset on do it with the best of your ability.

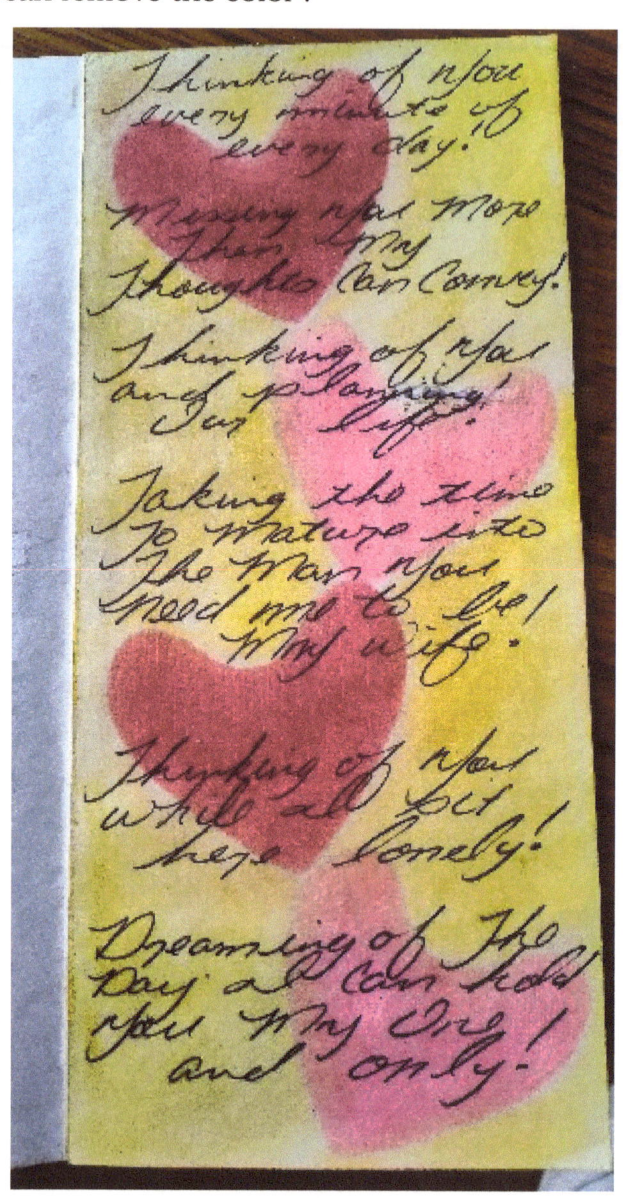

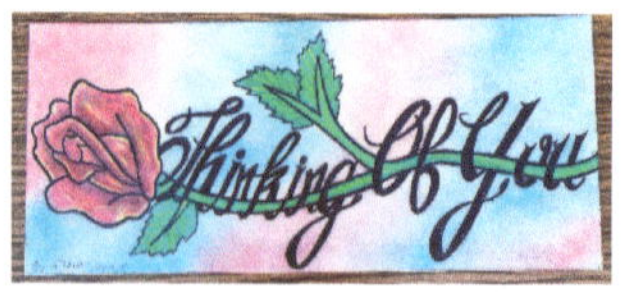

Chapter 10

Designs/Card Patterns

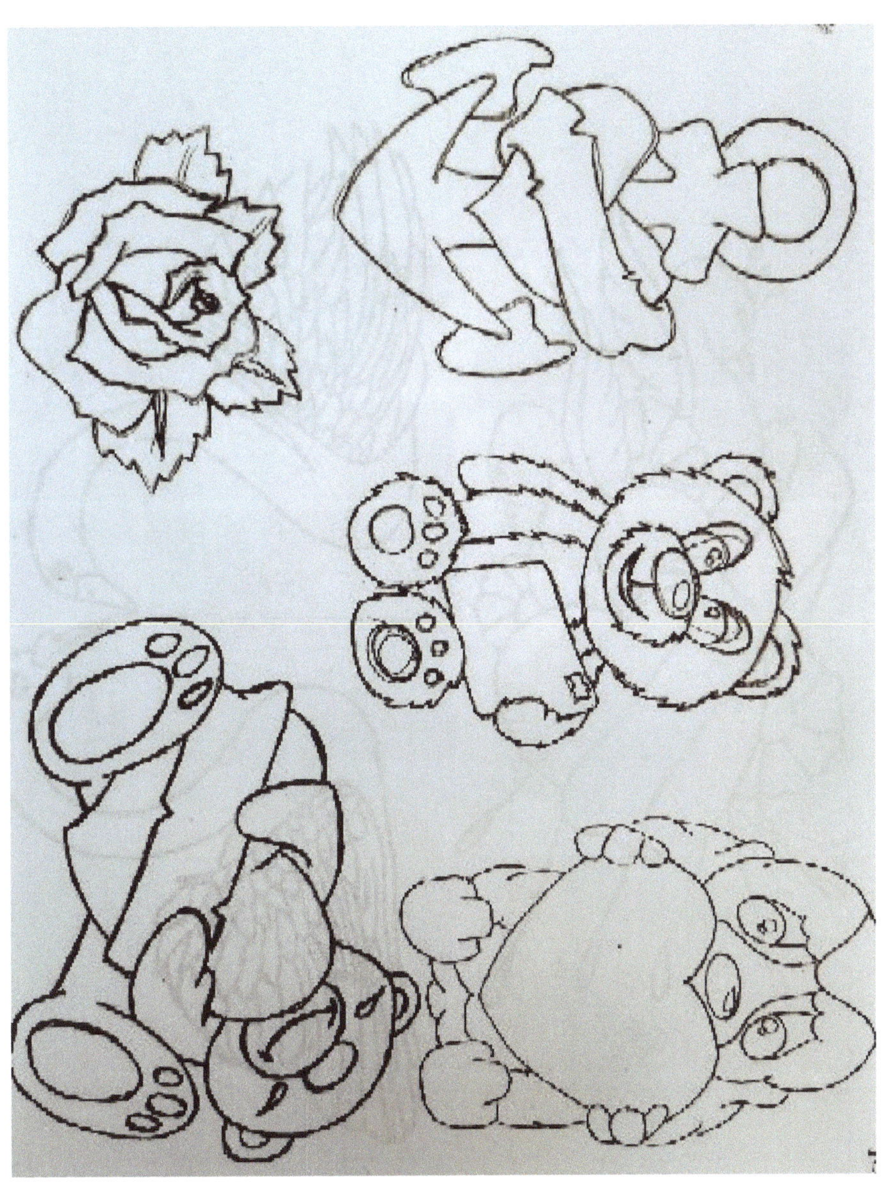

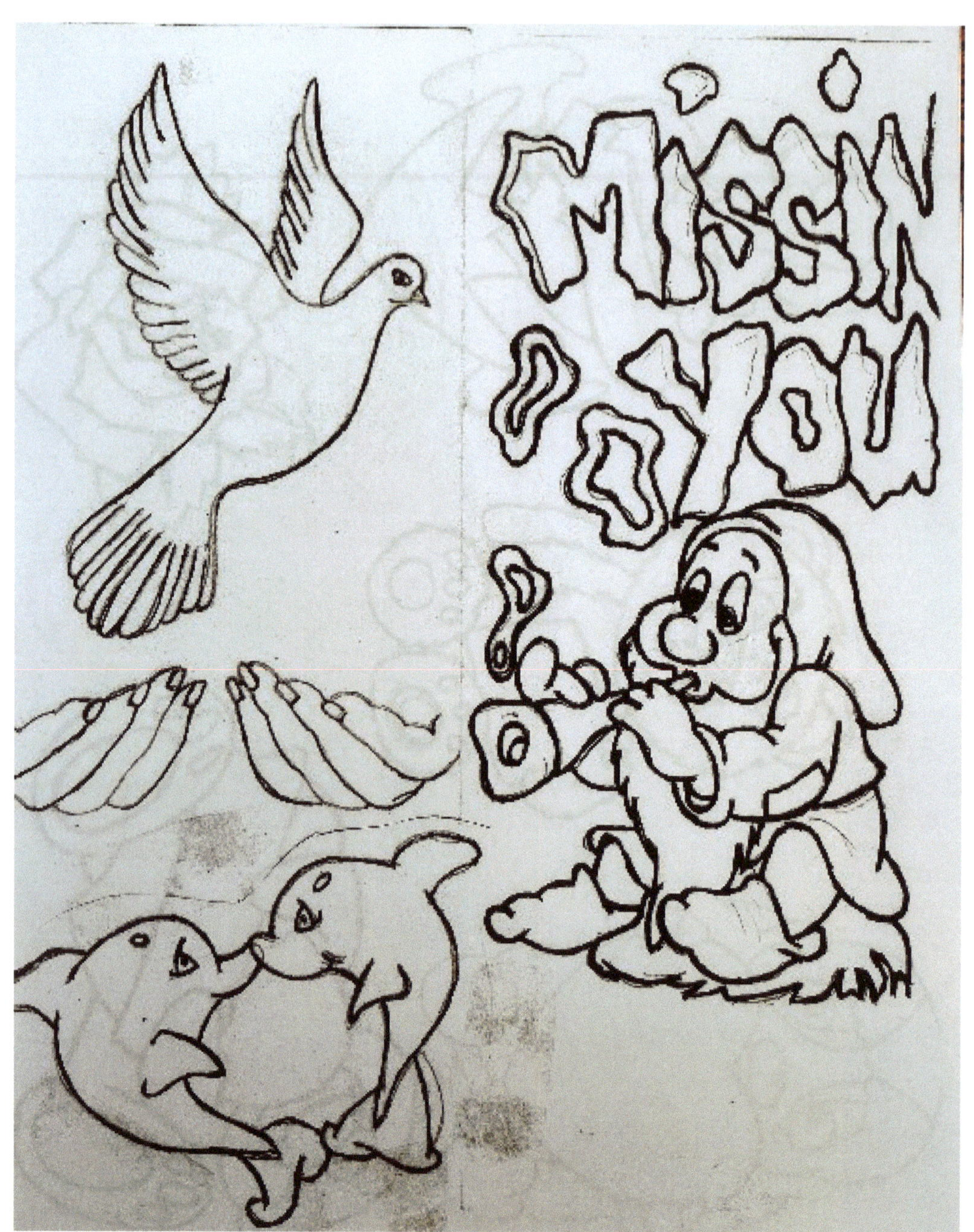
MISSIN
YOU

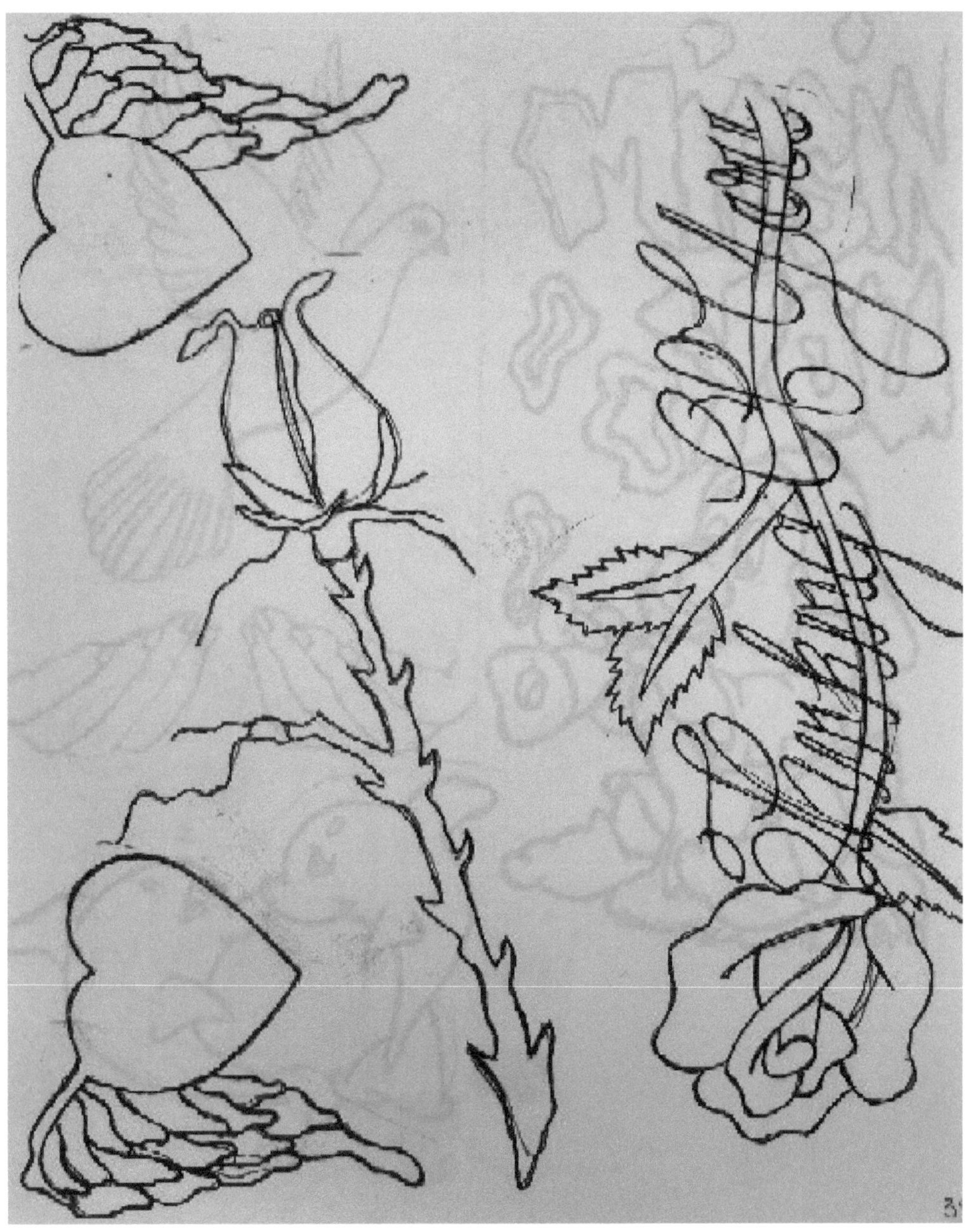

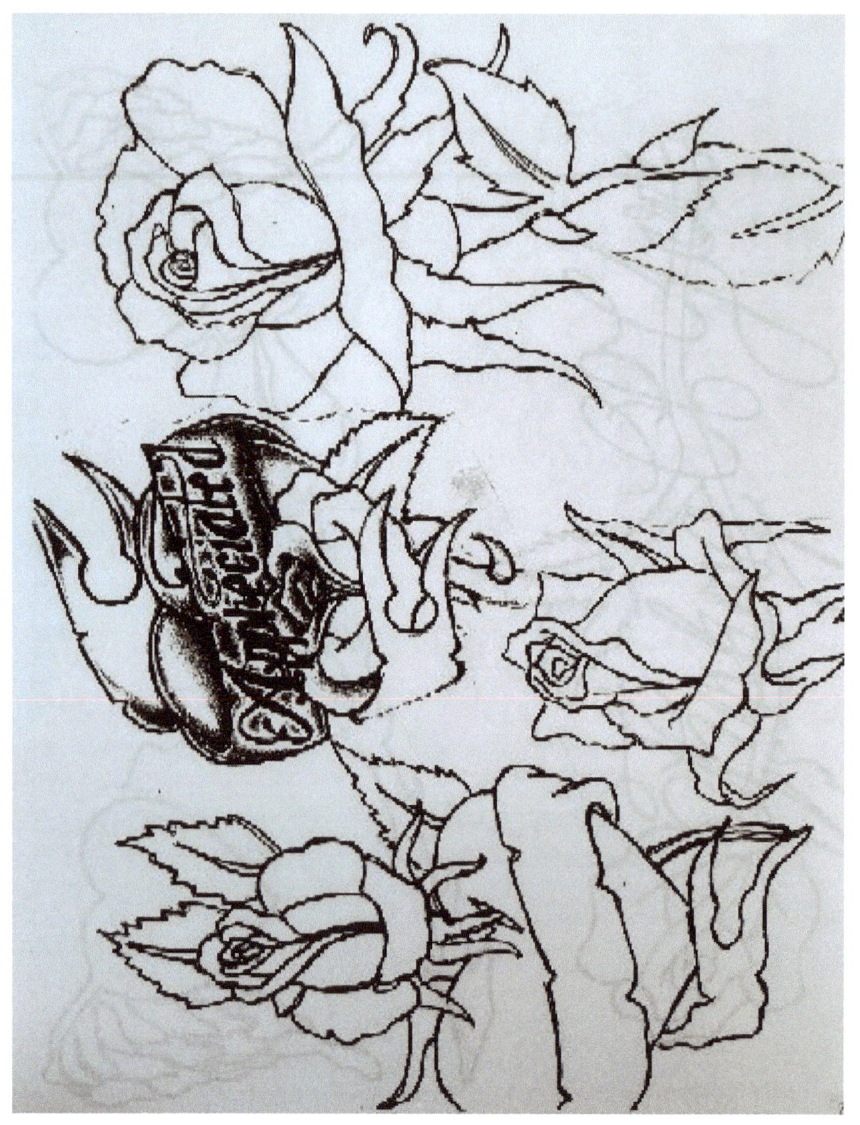

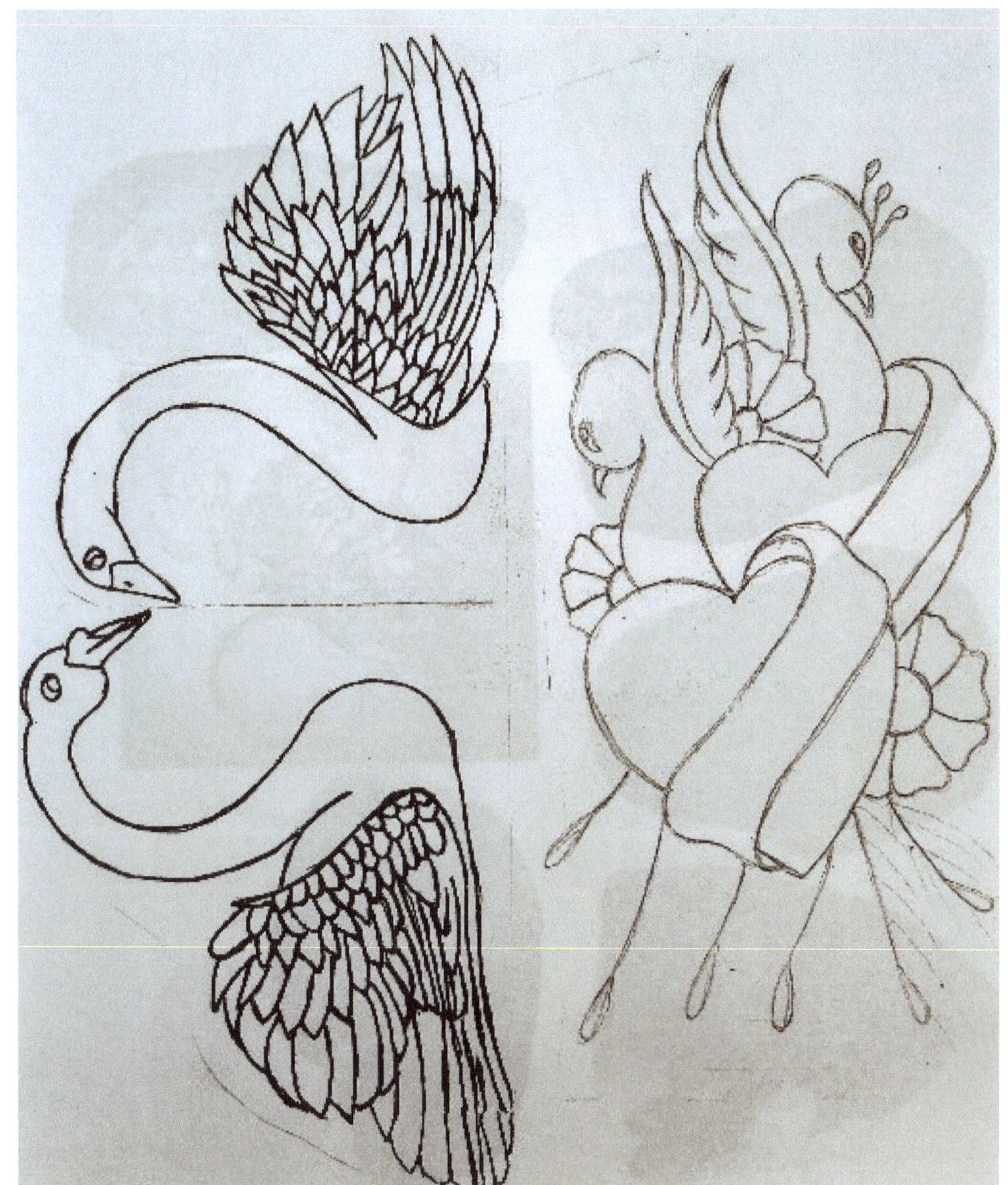

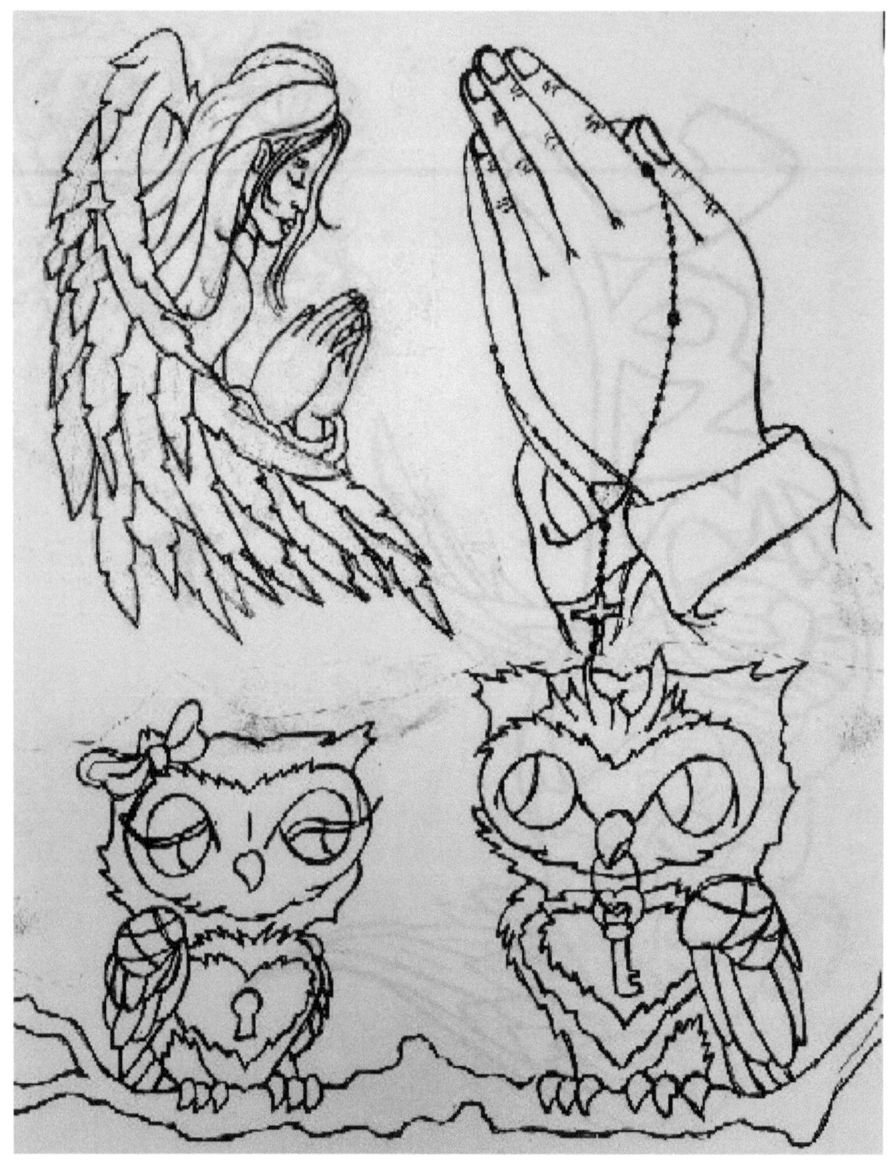

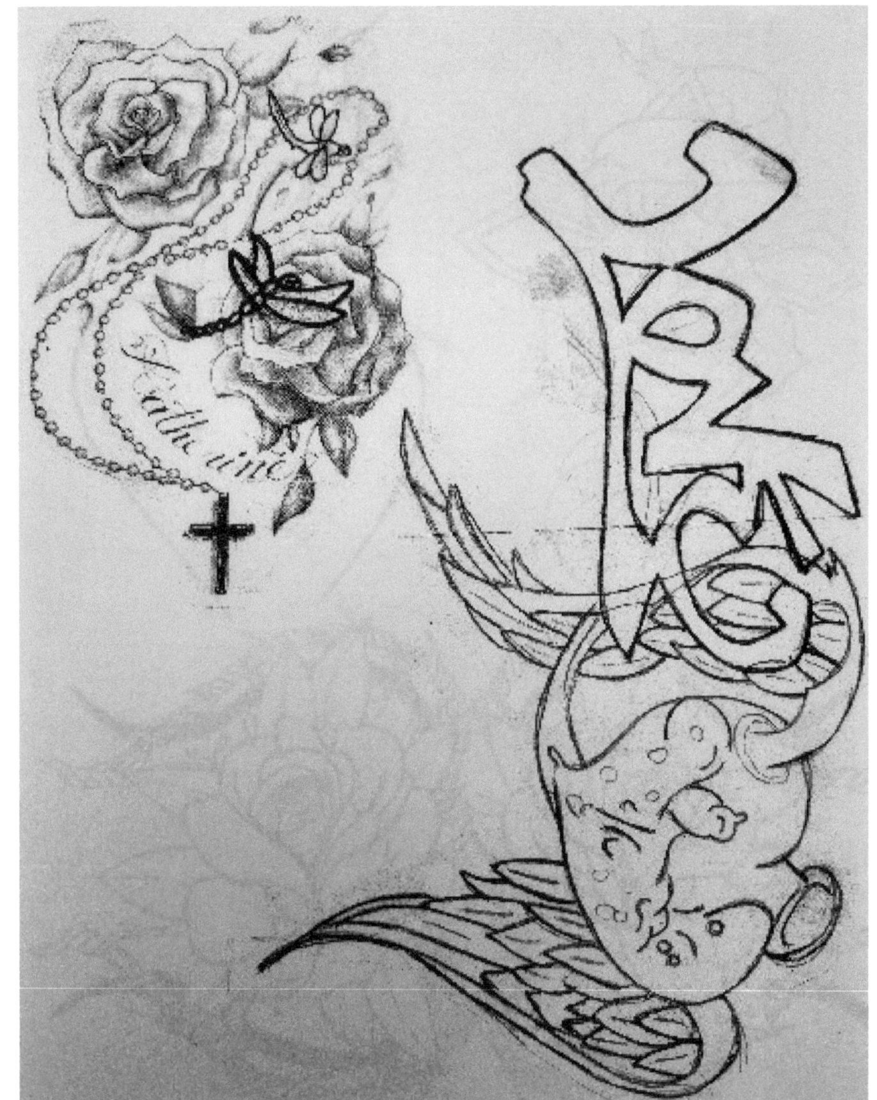

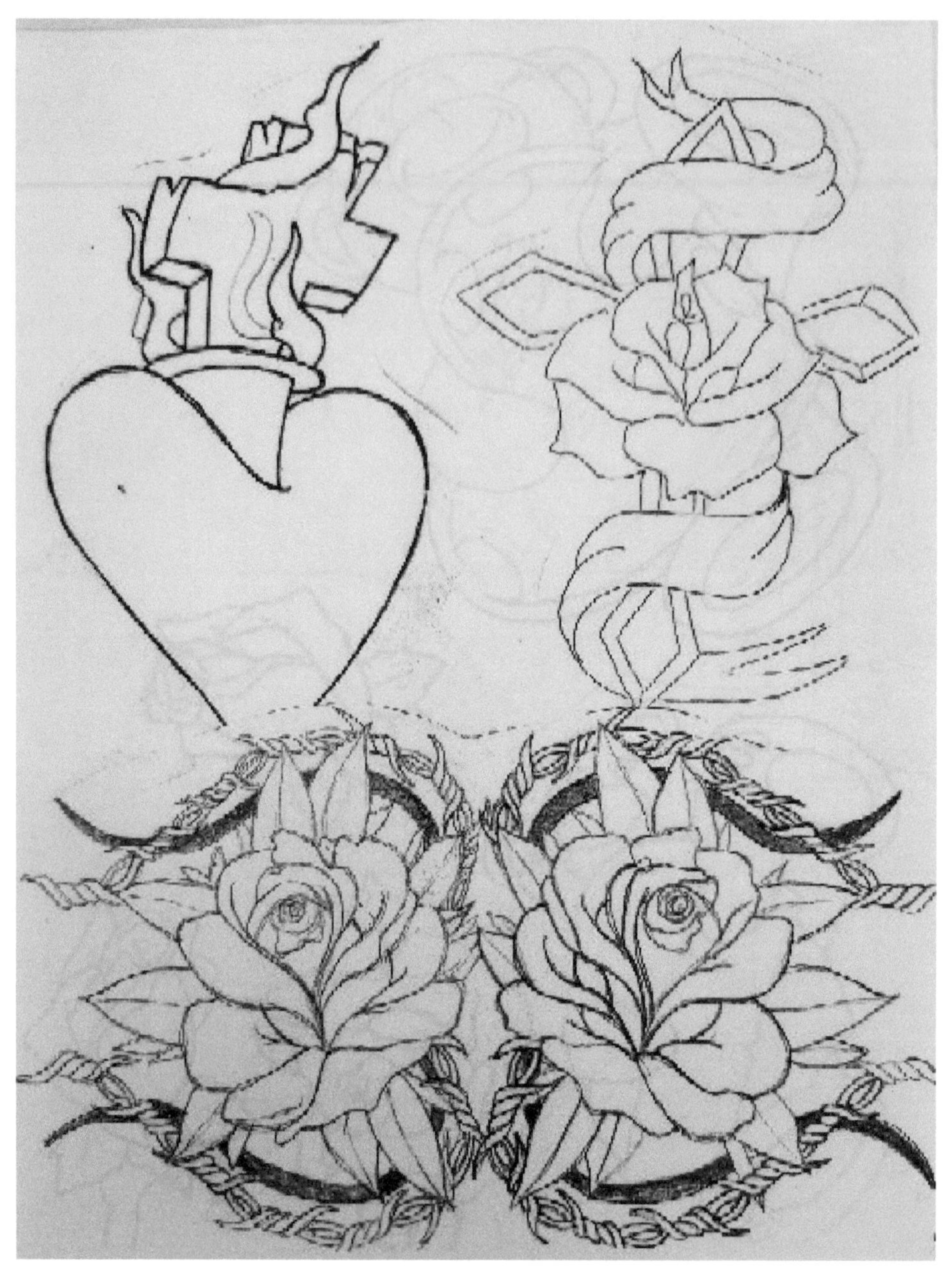

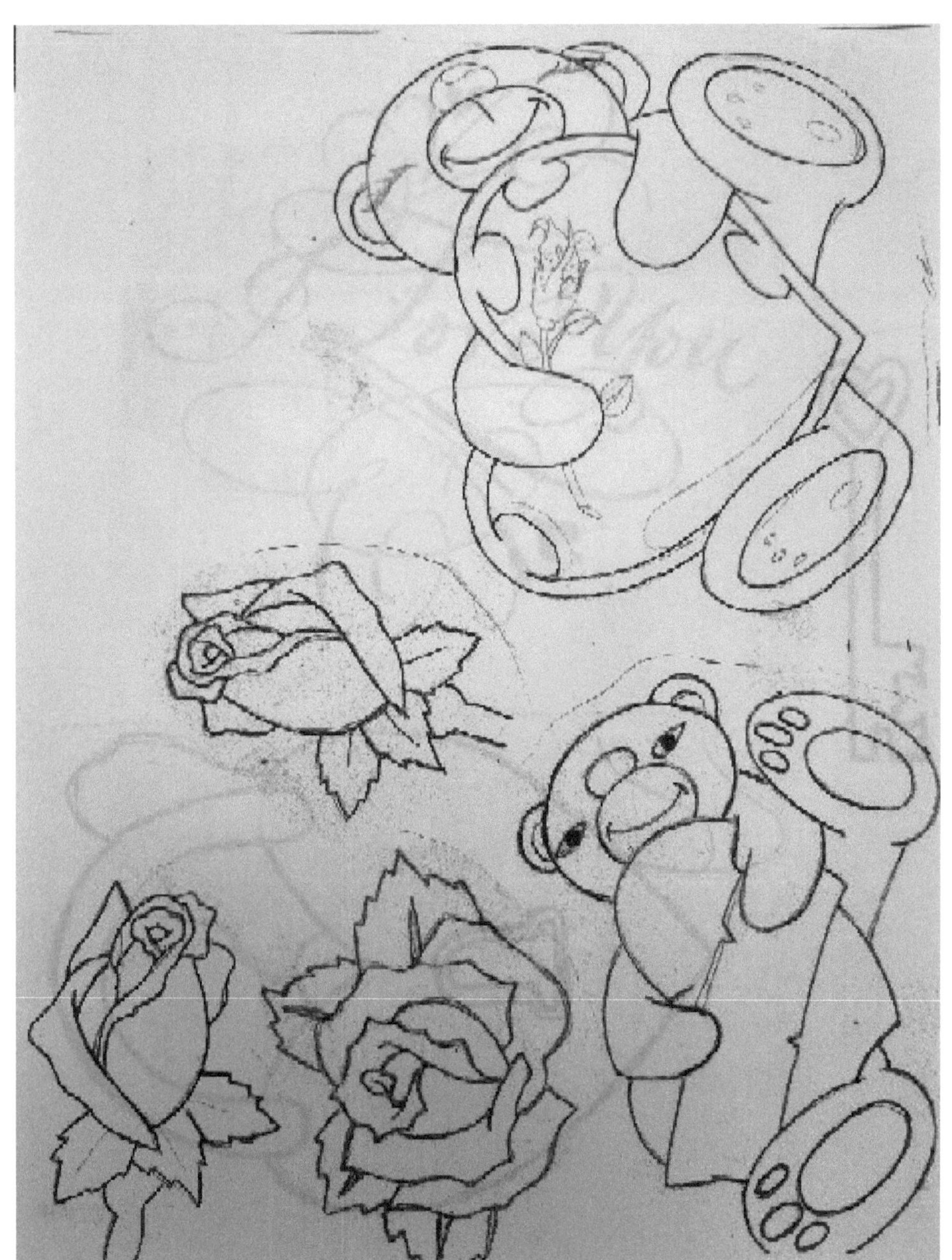

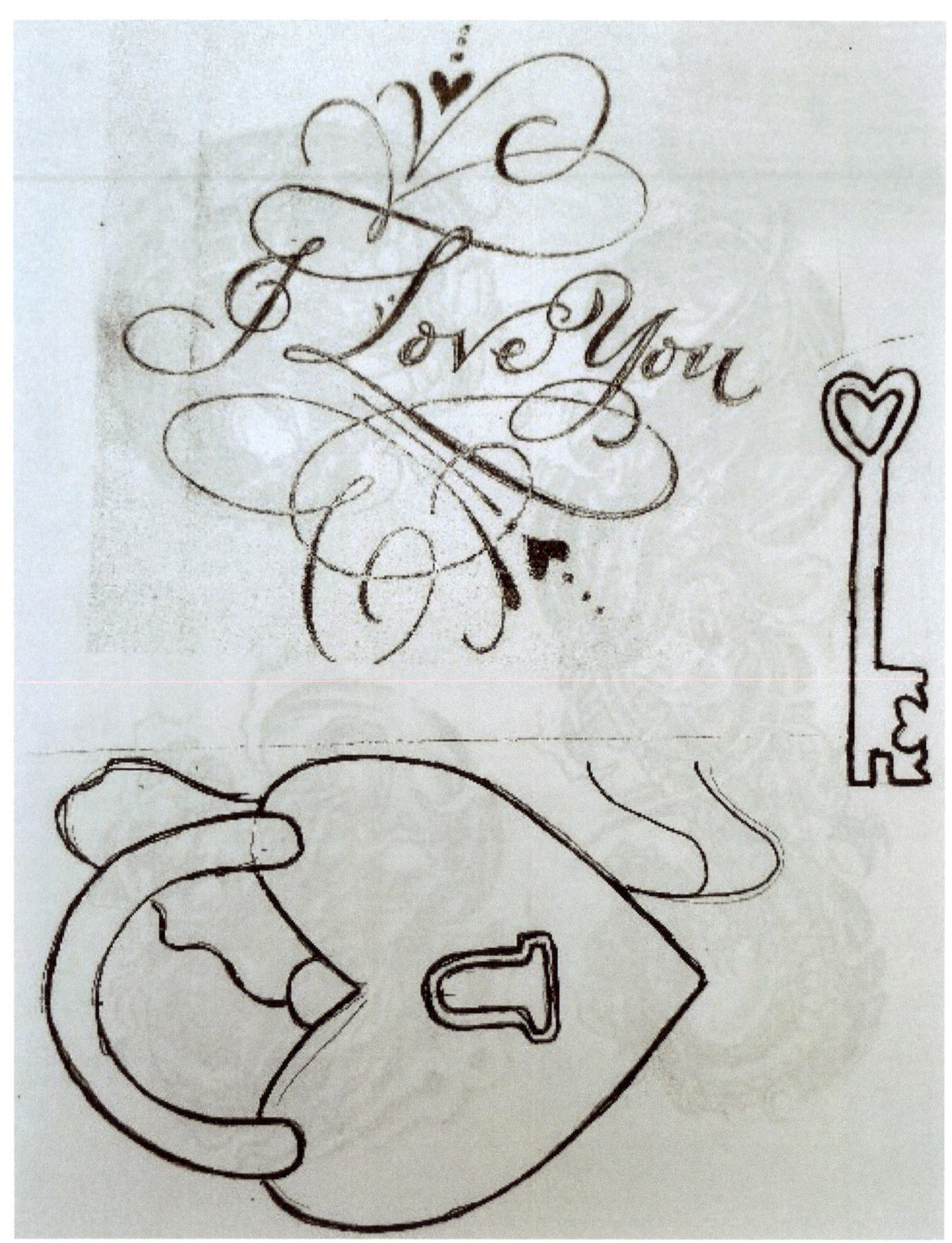

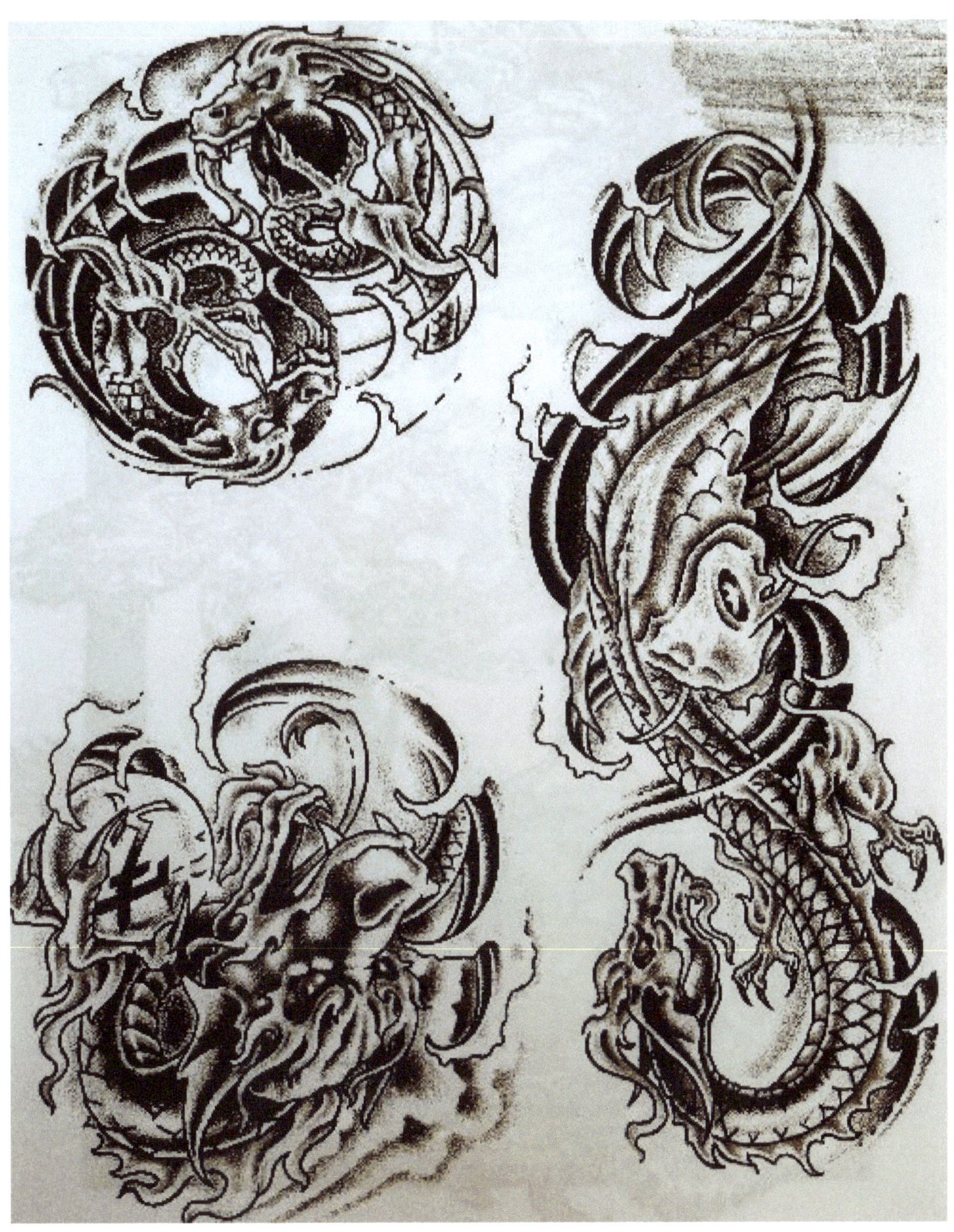

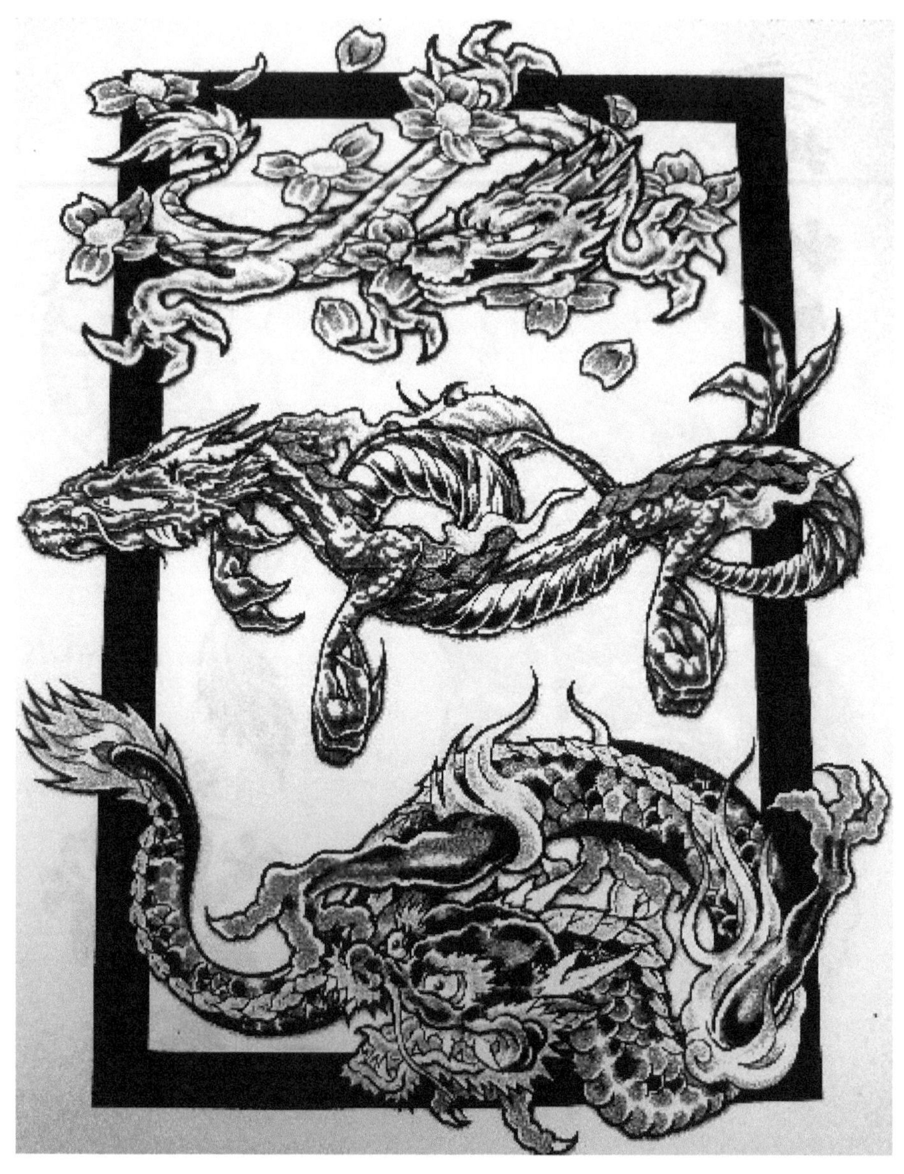

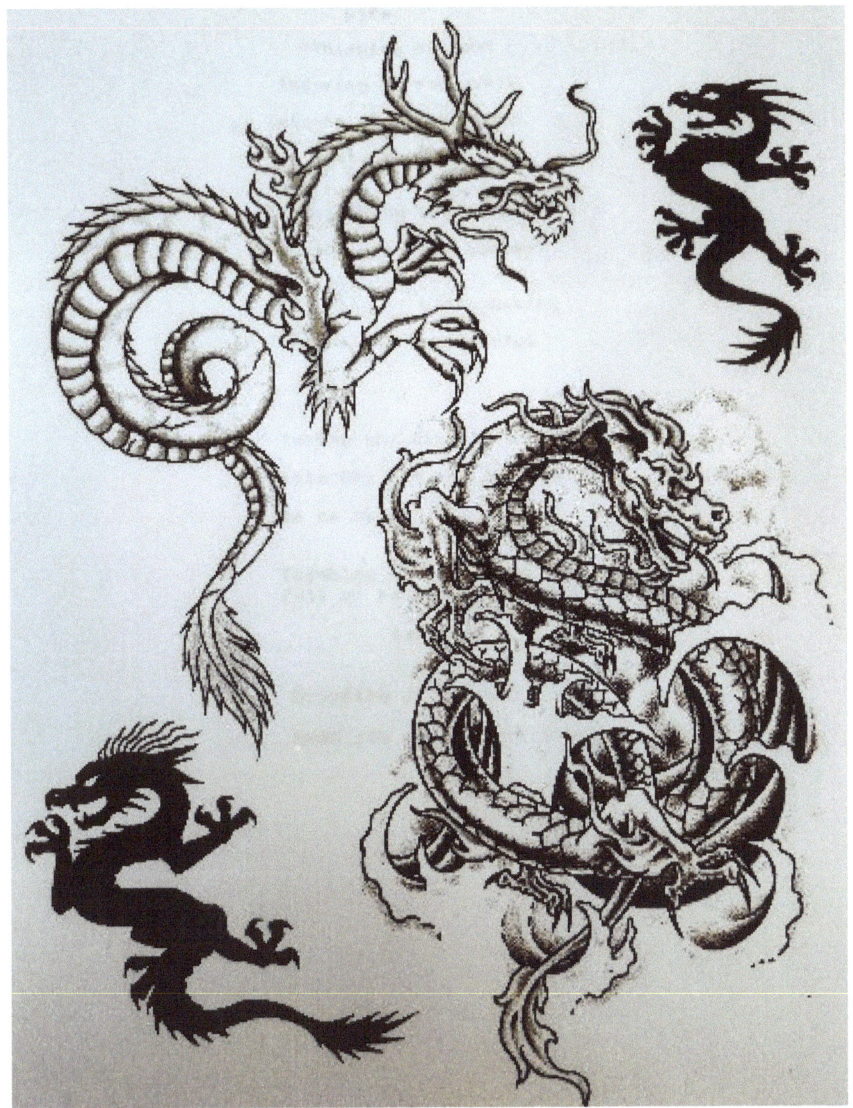

STENCILS

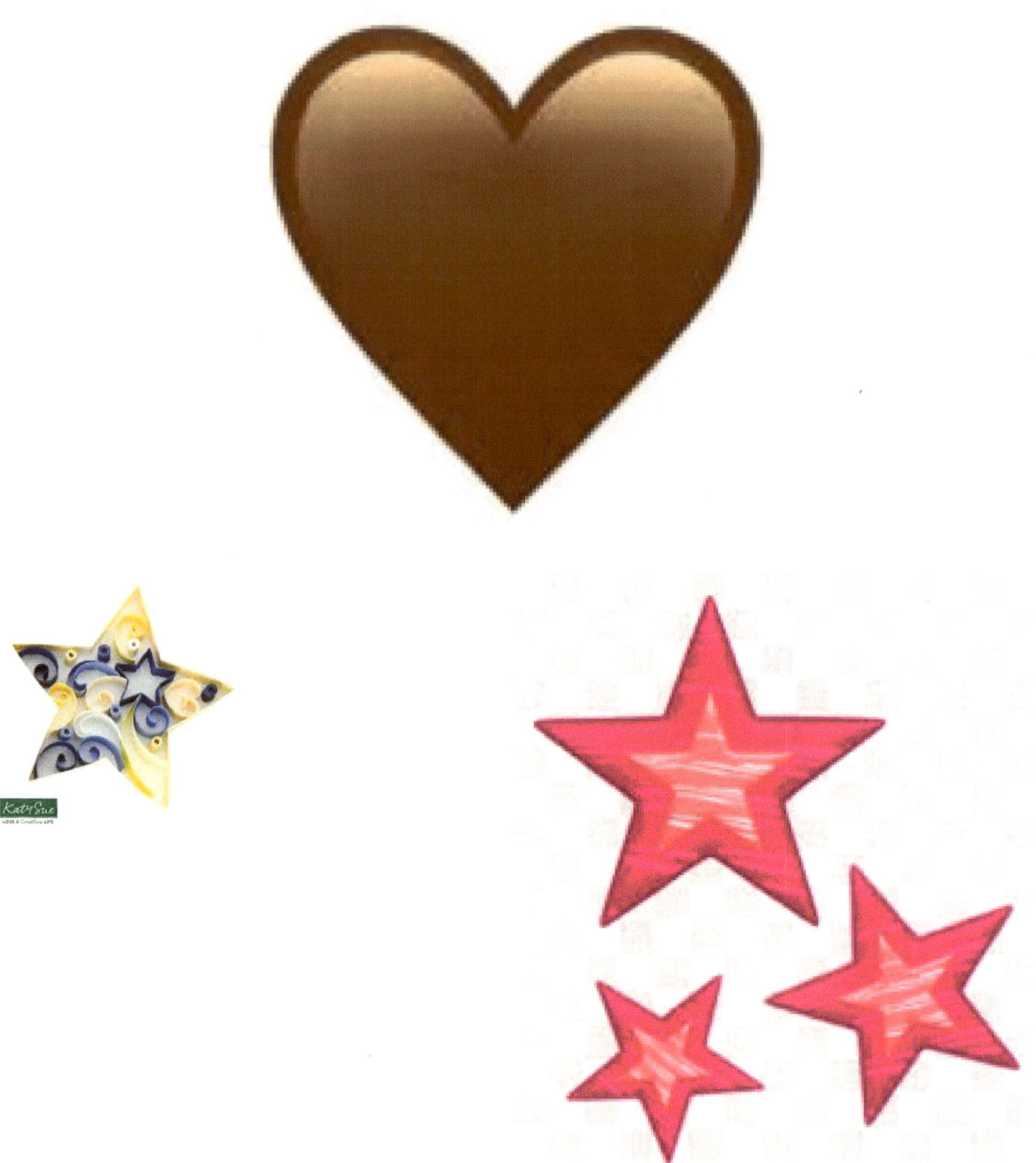

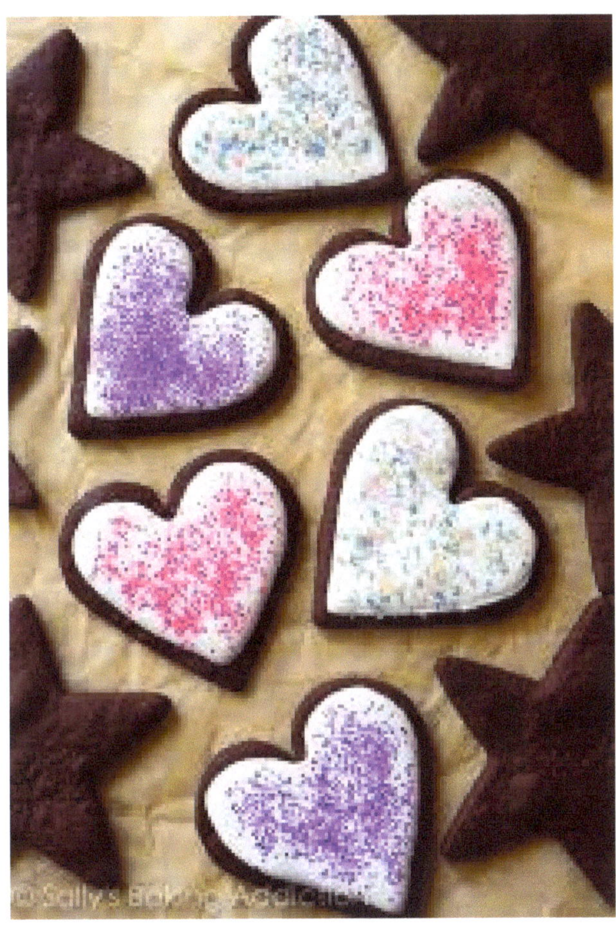

Chapter 11

Original Poetry

Wife
"Thinking of You"
Thinking of you every
minute of every hour
of every day!

Missing You more than
my thoughts can convey!

Thinking of You while making
plans for a wonderful
life!

Taking the time to mature
into the man you need me
to be my wife!
Thinking of you while I sit here
full of heartache and feeling lonely!
Dreaming of the day I can hold
my one and only!

Wife
"Then You Came Into My Life"
Just like Eeyore My life
has always been covered by
clouds of hopelessness and despair!

Like I am always about to fall
off of life's ledge and
happy days were rare!

Then You came into my life
and the clouds have begun to part
and the sun has started to shine in my life!

The day I realized I was not being pushed
off a ledge but was merely standing on a
rock was the day you said yes to becoming
my Wife!

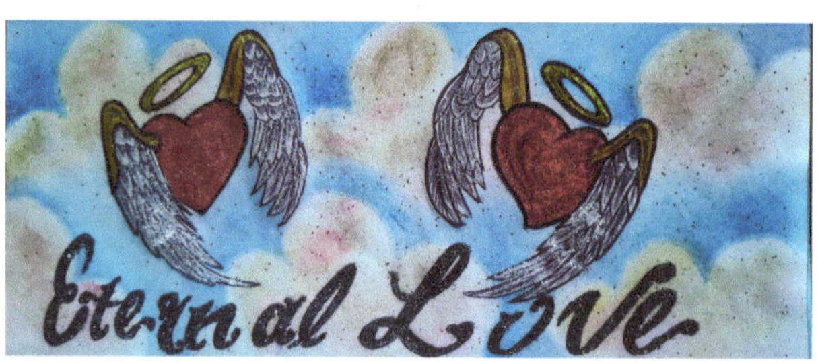

Wife
"More Precious"
You are more precious than
diamonds and more valuable
than gold!

You are my eternal soulmate
and I miss your touch truth
be told!

You are amazing you are
strong you are my life
words can not truly explain
what you mean to me my wife!

Thankyou for the way you love
me my Queen!

I will forever respect, honor, and
love you with every fiber of my being!

Wife/Girlfriend/Lover
"More Than Words"
I miss you more than
words can describe!

I know it has been tough
but true friendship
always survives!

I miss your touch
I miss your smile!

I love that even now
you go that extra mile!

I miss everything about
you my Queen!

I will forever love you
with every fiber of my being!

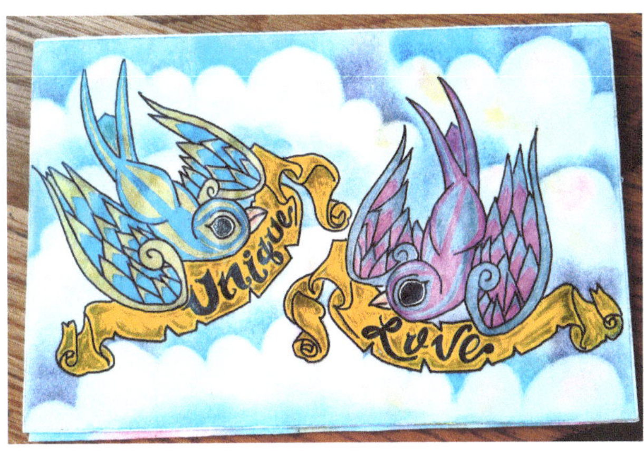

Mother
"Not a Day Goes By"
Mother not a day goes by
that you are not on my mind!

I want to thankyou for all the
sacrifices you have made and
still you make time after time!

Whenever I feel life has me on
the ropes!

I think of you because it is
your love that brings me hope!

Mother I don't think you truly
have a clue!

What you mean to me and
how much I love You!

Birthday/Mother
"My Present To You"
This special day comes
comes only once a year!

Mother truth be told
I wish I were there!

I want to bring a smile
to your face and to your
heart!

I know this time is
tearing you apart!

So my present to you is
maturing into the man you
always dreamed that I could be!

Mother I wish you the Happiest
Birthday and know I will love
you for all eternity!

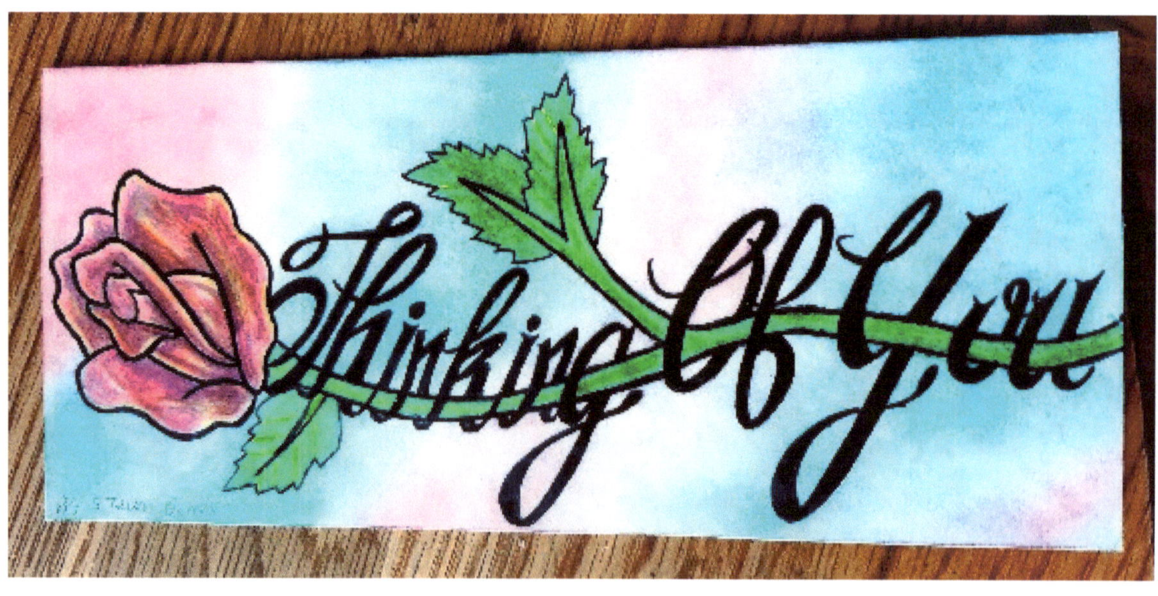

Mother
"I am Now Maturing"
Mother I can not put
into words what you
    mean to me!

Thankyou for always being
there when all I have caused
    is pain and misery!

Mother I am blessed
that you gave me life!

I know it is time
to grow up and to
quit living in strife!

I am maturing into the
man you always wanted
me to be!

From the bottom of my
heart I will love you for all
    eternity!

Anniversary/Mom and Dad
    "Golden Years"
    Mom and Dad
This special day comes
    only once a year!

    Truth be told I
    wish I was there!

    To see you in the
    glory of your
    golden years!

    Mom and Dad
    thankyou for always
    loving me and being there!

    You two are what true
    love is all about
    I must say!

I LOVE Y'ALL and
    wish you two a
Happy Anniversary!

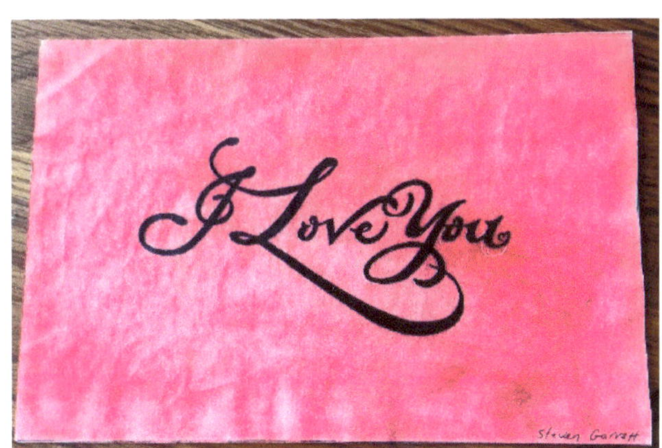

Daughter
"My Princess"
My Princess I am so
proud of the lady you
have grown to be!

You are smart, strong, and
best of all you have
    integrity!

As a Father I could
not have asked or prayed
for better children!

Yes you are truly
one in a million!

You are forever in
my heart and soul!

I am so grateful for you
and love you more than
you will ever know!

Daughter
"Baby Girl"
It won't be long until
Daddy can hold you in
    his arms!

Or tuck you in at night
and keep you free from
    harm!

I need you to be a big
girl and listen to your
    Mother!

You will always be our
Baby Girl there will
    never be another!

I will forever Love You
    Baby Girl!

I want you to know You will
    always be Daddies world!

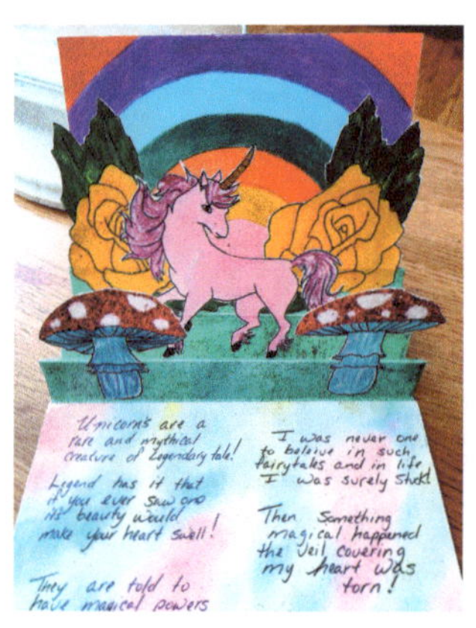

Son
"My Son"

My son I am so proud
you are growing into a
young man!

I want to give you a little
advice you need to set goals
and make future plans!

That way you know which
direction you are going in life!

It will save you a lot
of heart ache and strife!

My son you can always come to
me to get things off your chest!

Just know I will always love you
and that you are truly blessed!

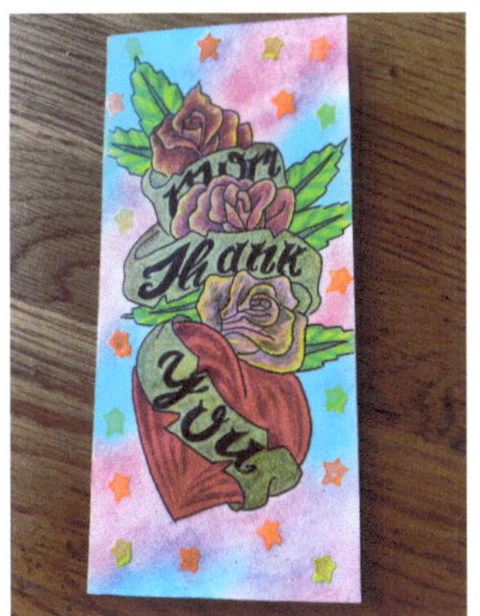

Son
"Little Superman"

I want you to know you
you are my little superman!

I need you to help your
Mother as much as you can!

I want you to know you are
in all my thoughts and in my
prayers!

Just because I am not at home
doesn't mean that I am not
thinking about you or that I care!

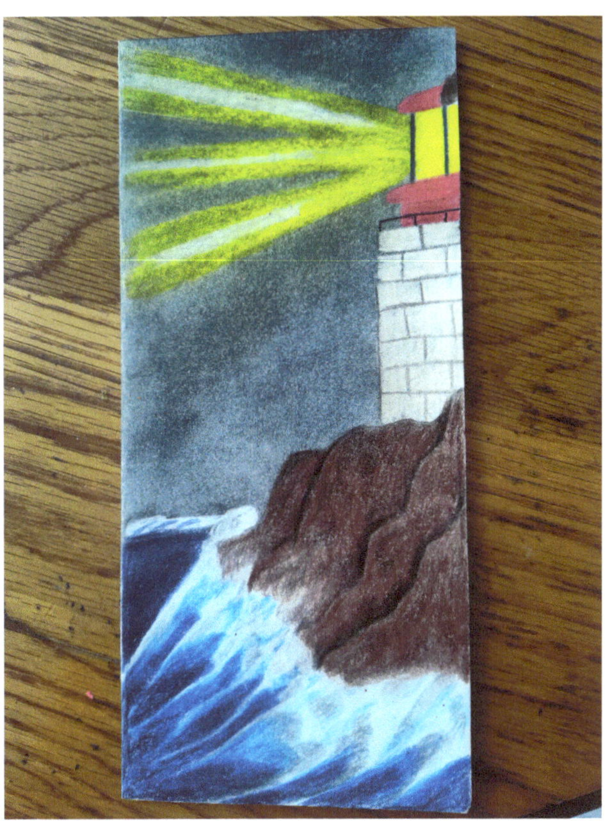

Friend
"Always Been"

I want you to know
You are in my thoughts
and prayers!

I truly do miss you
and truly do care!

You have always been there
through thick and thin!

You have always been
a true friend!

Thankyou for being the
person that you are!

I miss you with every
bear of my heart!

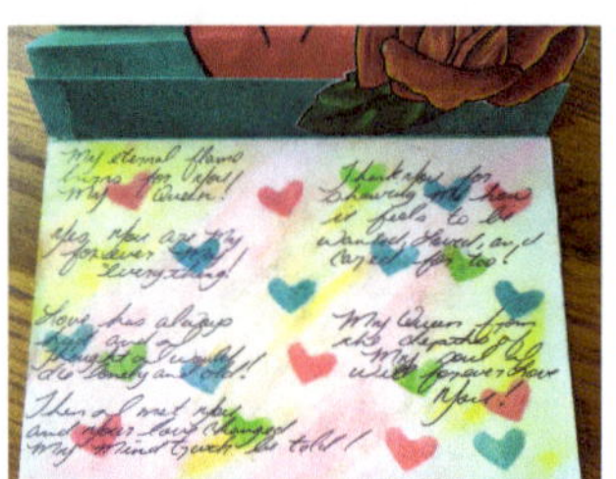

Friend
"Priceless"

I am sending you this
card to let you know you
 are on my mind!

Thankyou for remaining
my friend even after all
  this time!

Almost everybody has
wilted away but you
 have stayed loyal and
   true!

Your friendship is priceless
 and my life is better just
  knowing you!

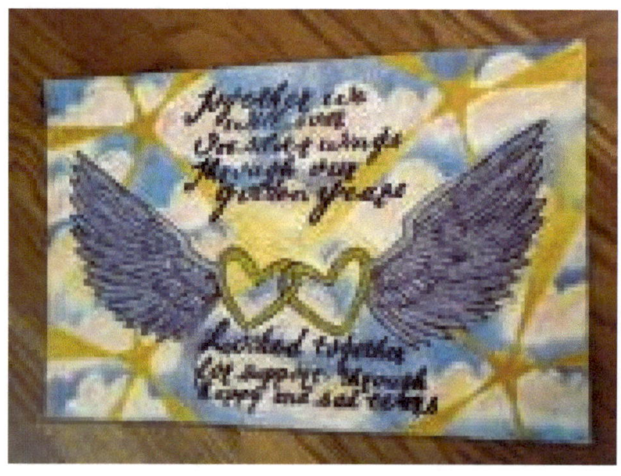

Love
"Love"

Love is more than
just a thought!

It is an action and a
feeling that means
         a lot!

Love is everlasting
forgiving and nurturing
        as well!

Love is willing to compromise
and also listening when you
have something to tell!

Love is totally selfless
and sacrificing too!

This is part of what
Love means to me so know
that I love you!

Love
"You! You!"

Who? Who?
   You! You!

I've stayed up night after
  night searching every
          tree!

Let me check the lock to
  your heart I think I have
         the key!

    Who? Who?
     You! You!

  I found the lock that
   my key will open up so
my search has come to an end!

I have finally found my soulmate,
  my confidant, and my bestfriend!

        Who? Who?
        YOU! YOU!

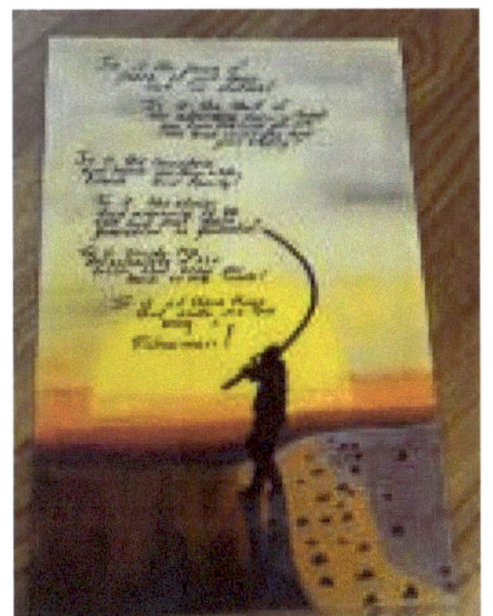

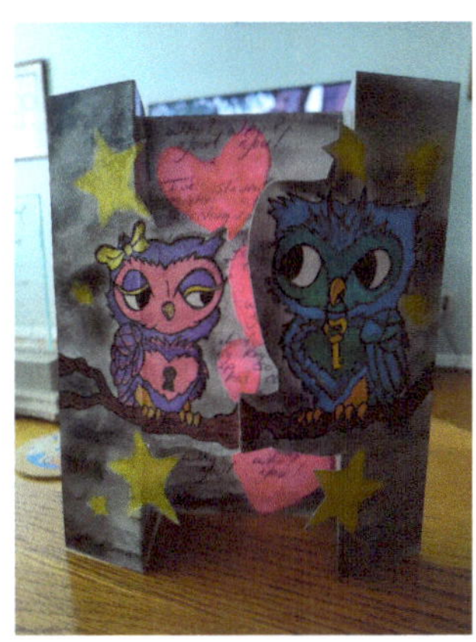

Epilogue/Positive Affirmation

First and foremost I want to thankyou for having a desire to make colorful heartfelt creations. Whether for loved ones or just to fill your locker box. It shows you have a desire for more than what is offered and that you have a drive which we all need to be productive in life.

Thankyou for choosing my book to help you on your card making journey. I hope and pray it was what you were looking for when you purchased it. I hope the descriptions truly helped to assist you in creating your own colorful creations , and that the examples gave you good visual depictions of what you were trying to create.

Most of all I hope you got a sense of accomplishment and a positive boost to your self esteem. If you are like me nothing in life has come easy. I used to make excuses why everything in my life was going wrong. I always blamed others for my problems never wanting to admit I was the problem. When I finally admitted to myself I was the problem I was finally able to start to rebuild myself.

This brought back dreams that I thought were gone never to be able to obtain. Dreams that I haven't had since I was seventeen. This first dream was just to have my family back in my life. It didn't happen overnight but slowly and with a lot of hard work these doors slowly started to crack open. The hardest work I had to do was looking into the depths of the monster that I created. To get to the heart of myself, my problems, my pain and the pain I had caused others. Once I found me again and re-centered who I was I could focus on clearing all the ashes of the burnt bridges to get to the foundations. So I could start to rebuild these meaningful relationships I dreamed about having with my family. It was the hardest most hurtful process I ever went through in my life. Seeing how bad I hurt the very ones I wanted back in my life. Four years later the rewards of this work started showing. When I started this process I had not heard from my Dad, brothers, my son, or had anyone who loved me not even myself for twenty five years or more. Now I have a beautiful wife, my mother, father, brothers and upon my release i will get my son back in my life. I can now look in the mirror and honestly say I love to the man looking back at me. The hard work i have put in has made me a man of integrity and accountability and has given me a new lease on life. It brings tears of joy to be able to share this with you. I hope it helps you in your life's journey.

Now I have always dreamed of writing my own book but never believed I was smart enough to accomplish this. Just know we can accomplish any goal we set are minds to. I will never let the devil steal another dream of mine or shatter any more relationships.

He has no more control over my life. So I challenge you to dare to dream because everyone even you no matter what you did in your past. Has the right to dream and you have something positive to offer the world!!!!!!!!!!!!

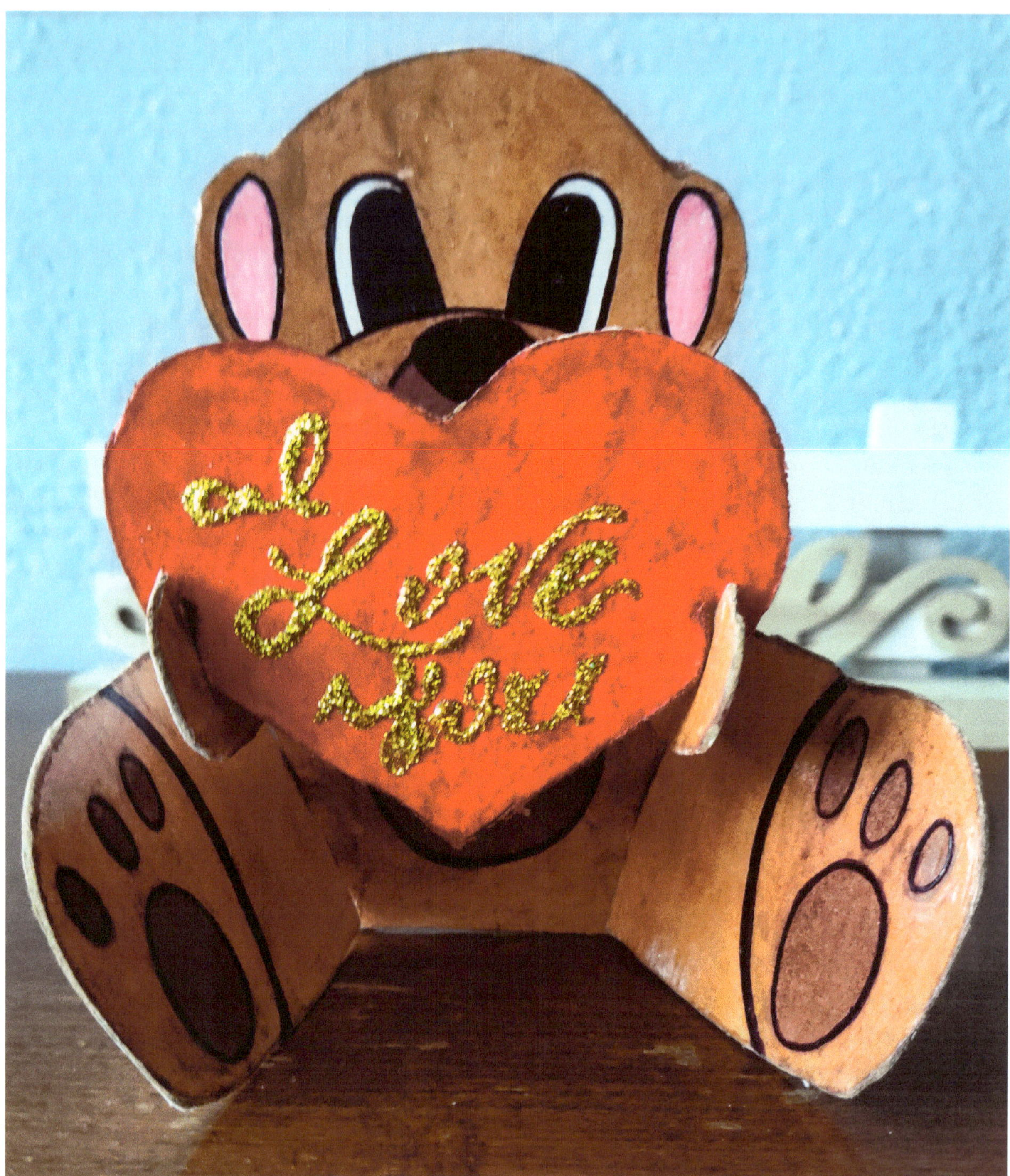

About the Author

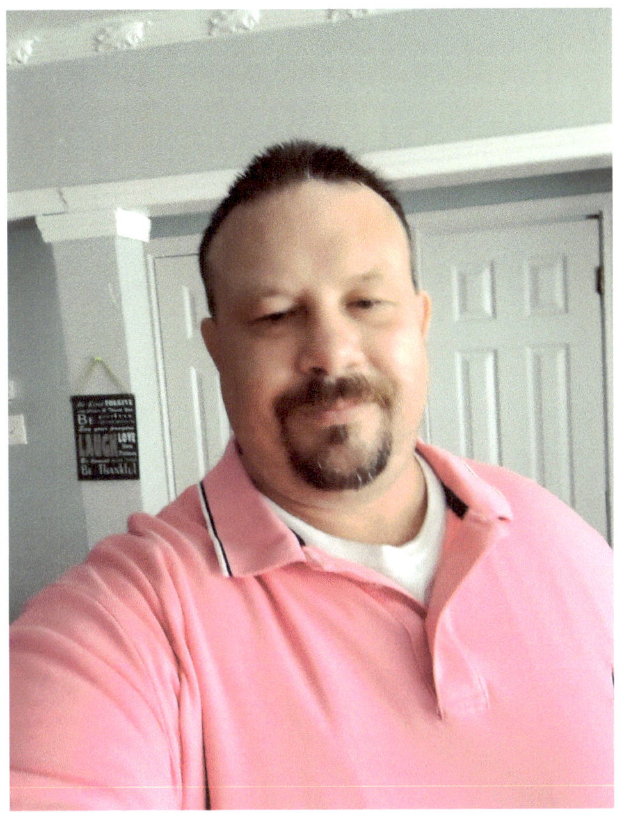

Steven Garrett is an artist a self published Author and an entrepreneur. He spent over twenty years in prison and is now dedicated to inspiring and helping others stay out. He has a powerful message of hope to inspire troubled youth. He was addicted to drugs and a life of crime. He found accomplishment and hope through these very cards.